101
WATER POLO
OFFENSIVE DRILLS

PETER J. CUTINO SR. and PETER J. CUTINO JR.

ISBN: 1-58518-314-8
Library of Congress Number: 00-108296

Book layout and cover design: Rebecca Gold
Drawings: Rosemarie Cutino Topper

Coaches Choice
P.O. Box 1828
Monterey, CA 93942
www.coacheschoiceweb.com

For more information about the drills in this book and waterpolo in general visit our website at www.waterpolo.cutino.com.

DEDICATION

This book is respectfully dedicated to the memory of
Coach Steve Heaston
(1946-1999)

ACKNOWLEDGMENTS

Over the years, special thanks are extended, to all of the players and coaches whom we have had the opportunity to work with, and compete against. The challenges created in water polo competition best describes the basis of what sports should be: To try to imbue a sense of honor, genuine team spirit, respect for opponents and to reflect the notable and noble sentiment of the human spirit in striving to attain a goal.

Peter J. Cutino Sr.
Peter J. Cutino Jr.

PREFACE

This book reflects a combined fifty years of coaching and thirty-five years of actual competition as players. Our experiences include every level of competition from age group and high school to collegiate and international competition. It is our intent to add to the information available for development of coach and player in the sport of water polo.

Peter J. Cutino Sr.
Peter J. Cutino Jr.

CONTENTS

Chapter 4: Individual Fundamentals of Shooting

DIAGRAM KEY

25m or 30m	25 or 30 meter course length
⊗	Offensive player with the ball
◯	Offensive player
X	Defensive player
◄───────	Movement of player
∧∧∧	Dribbler
- - - ◄ - - -	Movement of ball (pass)
◄───────	Shot

CHAPTER 1

INDIVIDUAL BALL HANDLING DRILLS

INTRODUCTION

INDIVIDUAL BALL HANDLING SKILLS

Individual offense means the ability of an individual to learn a variety of skills in order to facilitate the situations that occur in the game. The fundamentals of ball handling include many skills. Body coordination and mental alertness are often just as important as manual dexterity and hand-eye coordination.

Any ball handling drills must include proper positioning of the body – which encompasses body balance, timing and coordination. To be an effective ball handler, a player must be able to mentally anticipate where to be to receive or release a pass, to see the flow of the game and stay alert at all times. Just as in other sports that involve a ball, hand-eye coordination is vitally important. Ball handling drills must help improve the player's ability in areas such as lifting the ball, spinning the ball, receiving and passing the ball – both in the air or on the water – and overall ball control. These fundamentals must be mastered.

Without the ability to handle the ball and move it and the body into a position to get a pass off, no offense can be effective. The ability to react correctly and quickly to each new situation that rises involves a number of different skills that often take years to fully learn. While there are a wide variety of passing and shooting skills necessary for water polo, it is better to be able to do a few "really well" than many at a mediocre level.

#1 HAND DRILLS

Objective: To improve coordination and feel for the ball.

Description: Players practice a series of hand drills:

- Player tips the ball in the air using only the finger tips, with arms straight (to strengthen the fingers).
- Player picks up the ball with the back of the one hand and then rolls the ball onto the palm of the same hand (to improve "feel" and coordination).
- Player squeezes a slippery ball, causing it to "pop up," then catch it again.
- Player rolls his hands over the ball until thumb is under the ball (to simulate the technique for a back-hand pick-up).
- Player keeps rolling the ball, with alternate hands to keep the ball spinning.

Variation: Drills should be done both right and left hand.

Coaching Point:

- These hand drills can be done during leg conditioning.

#2 FACING FORWARD WITH BALL OVERHEAD DRILL

Objective: To improve ball handling skills while developing stamina and leg strength.

Description: The player keeps the ball overhead, while passing it from left hand to right and right hand to left. While keeping his arms straight and not looking at the ball, the player must "walk 25-to-30 meters" using the eggbeater kick.

Variation: Perform same drill while going backwards and sideways.

Coaching Points:

- This drill can be done single-file or in groups.
- The coach should strongly emphasize players keeping their arms straight.

#3 MOVING BALL SIDE-TO-SIDE DRILL

Objective: To improve ball handling skills while developing stamina, leg strength and balance in the water by using scissor kicks.

Description: The player swims 25 or 30 meters using scissor kicks while transferring the ball from one hand to the other.

Variations: The player moves the ball to the opposite side, releases the ball, then picks up the ball with the opposite hand and repeats. The player moves the ball to the opposite side without releasing the ball — until the ball is actually transferred to the opposite hand.

Coaching Point:

- Hand positions, while picking up the ball, can be from either under the water, or by placing the hand over the ball. The coach should dictate which technique to use. (In young players, it is preferable to use the technique of picking the ball up from under the water.)

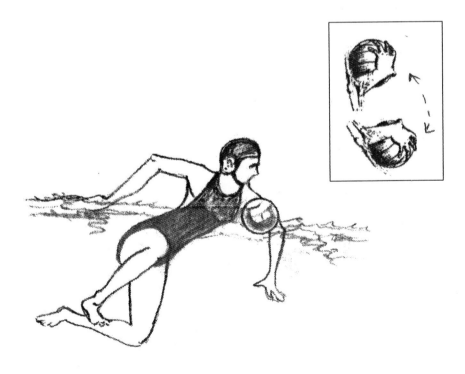

#4 DRIBBLE, SHOOT DOWN ON WATER DRILL

Objective: To improve ball handling skills while conditioning legs.

Description: The player dribbles the ball, picks it up and stretches high over his head, then shoots the ball down on the water (actually pounding the ball down to the water).

Variation: Player practices the drill using the opposite hand.

Coaching Point:

- This drill can be done single-file or in groups.

#5 DRIBBLE, FAKE SHOT, DRIBBLE DRILL

Objective: To improve ball handling skills.

Description: The player dribbles the ball, picks it up to shooting position, pumps as if to shoot, then puts the ball back in water and dribbles. Drill is repeated for 25 or 30 meters.

Variation: Player does the same drill using the opposite arm.

Coaching Points:

- This drill can be done single-file or in groups.
- Coach should emphasize that players fake with their body and not bring the ball forward.

#6 SELF PASS, SWIM AND CATCH DRILL

Objective: To improve ball handling skills and body balance.

Description: The player must toss the ball into the air, then take three arm strokes and catch the ball dry. The player then dribbles and repeats the drill for 25 or 30 meters.

Coaching Point:

- This is very a difficult drill that only the most experienced players will be able to master.

#7 DRIBBLE, STOP AND MAKE QUARTER TURNS DRILL

Objective: To improve ball handling and change of direction as well as starting and stopping skills.

Description: The player begins dribbling, stops and makes a quarter turn to the left and stops again. Continue making quarter turns and stops until facing original direction, then dribble and repeat drill three times in 25 or 30 meters.

Variations: The player performs the same drill but rotates to the right using the left hand. Drill can also be done to the draw side, using right hand to spin to the right and left hand to spin to the left.

Coaching Points:

- This drill will require players to use their legs effectively by drawing them up, underneath their body while turning.

- Emphasize letting go of the ball at every stopping point, then picking it up again.

- Handle the ball, do not grab it.

#8 HAND TO FOOT, FOOT TO HAND DRILL

Objective: To improve ball handling skills while enhancing hand-eye and body coordination.

Description: The players, from a layout position and while swimming on their backs, pass the ball from their right hand to their right foot. The right foot kicks the ball to their left hand, and it is then passed to the left foot to be kicked back to the right hand. This drill is repeated for 25 or 30 meters.

Coaching Point:

- This drill, and others that involve moving, passing, and moving with the ball will help the players with their coordination and balance in the water.

CHAPTER 2

PASSING DRILLS

INTRODUCTION

PASSING

One common characteristic that outstanding teams possess over other teams is pinpoint accuracy in their passing. The ability to execute good passes, both short and long, is often the difference between winning and losing. Passing must be emphasized in all training sessions.

Coaches should constantly look for and encourage proper passing techniques during practice sessions. Insisting that players consistently make good passes is vital for both individual and team development. It is imperative that each player be able to consistently execute good passes under varying conditions. Each coach should structure passing drills that will be the most beneficial for his particular team.

Good passers should be recognized during practice, so players will develop pride in that part of the game. At times, an entire training session should be devoted to just passing and shooting. During the off season, it is recommended that one day each week be devoted to passing and shooting only. In regular practices, normally twenty to forty percent of practice should be devoted to passing.

To catch the ball, the fingers should be relaxed, spread wide and slightly bent. Rather than stop the ball, continue to move in the direction of the received pass. The hand bends back at the wrist, with an easy movement of the elbow or shoulder.

#9 100 CONSECUTIVE DRY PASSES DRILL

Objective: To improve passing and ball handling skills while emphasizing pressure passing and the importance of "catching the ball."

Description: Two players start four meters apart, facing each other, and pass the ball back and forth. They must complete twenty dry passes before they can move to the next distance and begin again. At each successive distance (6m, 8m, 10m, 15m) they must complete twenty dry passes before moving farther apart. If the ball is dropped or the pass is uncatchable, the players must restart their count.

Variations: The coach can specify all right or left-handed catches. Another variation requires that passes from eight meters or less must be thrown with the non-shooting arm. Players can also receive a pass, turn away from the teammate, put the ball on the water, then turn and pass again.

Coaching Points:

- This drill is simple in concept, but extremely important. Put additional pressure on the players by having them count out loud the number of completed passes.

- This drill can be a contest to see which pair finishes first.

#10 PASS AND THREE STROKES DRILL

Objective: To improve passing skills while emphasizing movement after the pass.

Description: The players pair up anywhere in the pool, and pass the ball to each other, always swimming three strokes immediately after each pass.

Variations: The number of players on a ball can vary from two to four, and passes can be wet or dry.

Coaching Point:

- Players should strive for constant motion. This drill will help make the concept of constant motion become automatic to the players.

#11 MOVING 25 OR 30 METER BALL HANDLING DRILL

Objective: To improve passing and ball handling skills while conditioning legs.

Description: The players go through a series of ball handling drills as team-mates pass the ball to each other while they continue to move 25 or 30 meters and return. This can be a large group exercise. Each of the following passing drills cover a 25 or 30 meter distance:

- Right hand to left hand of partner and reverse coming back.
- Two balls passed at the same time.
- Two balls passed alternately.
- Two handed pass overhead, with high intensity.

Variations: Additional passing techniques can be incorporated, i.e., wet then dry backhands, 180- and 360-spins going both right and left.

Coaching Point:

- This drill is a good warm-up drill to use early in practice sessions.

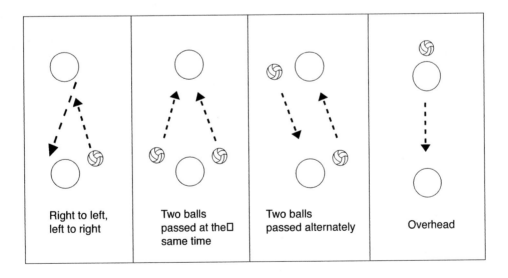

| Right to left, left to right | Two balls passed at the same time | Two balls passed alternately | Overhead |

#12 SEESAW PASSING DRILL

Objective: To improve passing skills while emphasizing that players come up out of the water to receive and pass the ball.

Description: Two players start four meters apart, facing each other, and pass after coming up out of the water as high as possible. The player receiving the pass then comes up as high as possible to catch the pass, goes down into the water, then comes up again to throw the next pass.

Variations: Each player must stay up as he catches and passes the ball. Right or left-handed passes and catches may be specified. This can also be a turn-and-pass drill performed in groups.

Coaching Point:

- This drill is meant to emphasize "high" water polo and is an excellent leg conditioner.

#13 BACKHAND-TO-BACKHAND PASSING DRILL

Objective: To improve passing and ball handling skills while emphasizing pressure passing and the importance of catching the ball.

Description: Two players start four-to-six meters apart, with their backs to each other, and catch and pass backhanded. Distance can vary depending on the ability of the players. Each dry pass should be caught backhanded with the receiver turning with the momentum of the ball. The ball is then put down on the water. The passer will gently press the ball down, while turning their palm under the ball and outward. Start each pass by moving the shoulders, then the arm, elbow and wrist. Aim with the wrist and end up facing the elbow.

Variations: This drill can be done with all right- or left-handed catches. Also, passes from eight meters or less can be done with the non-shooting arm. Allowing only dry catches and passes is another variation.

Coaching Points:

- This drill is a good way to lead up to proper backhand shots.
- Emphasize high elbow position.

#14 POP-UP PASS AND RETURN DRILL

Objective: To improve pop-up passing skills while swimming across the pool. This drill also helps with leg conditioning and ball handling.

Description: This drill is a series of passing and ball handling exercises performed while players swim 25 or 30 meters and return. This drill can be used for large groups. Player two, swimming in front, rolls on his back and catches the ball from player one, who uses a pop-up pass (while swimming, one hand lifts the ball from underneath while the other hand hits the ball with fingers and/or fingertips) to player two's right hand. Player two then passes a wet pass back to player one, who dribbles, then uses a pop-up pass to player two's left hand. The drill continues for the 25 or 30 meters.

Variations: The players switch positions when they reach the other end of the pool. Drill can also be performed using wet passes forward and dry backhand passes backwards.

Coaching Points:

- Demand accurate passing and continuous swimming.
- When performing a pop-up pass, the striking arm's elbow must be high.

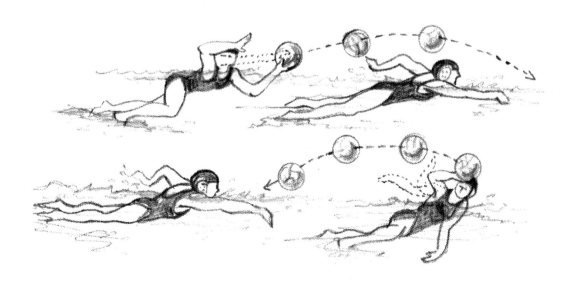

#15 THREE-MAN PASS SWIM DRILL

Objective: To improve passing and ball handling skills while emphasizing mobility, ball recognition and conditioning.

Description: Player one, swimming behind, passes the ball over the head of player two who is swimming on his back. Player two rolls onto stomach to see and receive the wet pass, turns and then continues to dribble to the opposite side. Meanwhile, player three begins swimming in the opposite direction and receives the ball in the same manner from player two, who changed directions after reaching the side. Player one continues the drill, receiving a wet pass from player three. This drill is similar to a weave in basketball.

Variations: Coach can have players use a variety of passes, including dry, pop-up, backhand, and spin-and-roll passes.

Coaching Point:

- This drill can be done quickly with high intensity, or in three-minute intervals.

#16 AMBIDEXTROUS PASSING DRILL

Objective: To practice ambidextrous passing while improving body balance and receiving techniques.

Description: Three players line up in a row. The player on the right passes to the right hand of the middle player who then passes to the player on the left. Player on the left then passes to the left hand of the middle player who passes to the player on the right. Players continue passing back and forth in this manner until they switch positions every four minutes.

Variation: The player in the center faces the opposite way.

Coaching Point:

- This drill is designed to encourage soft, accurate passing and receiving techniques.

#17 FACE-OFF REACTION DRILL

Objective: To teach players to anticipate, react quickly and aggressively retrieve the ball. (Very competitive)

Description: This drill involves two players positioned side-by-side who attempt to gain possession of the ball after the coach throws the ball between them (jump ball).

Variation: The player who gains possession of the ball attacks the goal with a drive-in shot. Sometimes the ball can be thrown in the air and favor one player or the other.

Coaching Point:

- This is meant to be an aggressive drill — emphasizing quickness, position, balance and control.

#18 PASS-AND-GO TECHNIQUE DRILL

Objective: To practice getting past an overly aggressive defensive player.

Description: The player with the ball rolls to his back allowing the defensive player to move up to block or inhibit the shot or pass. The offensive man sinks slightly, allowing the momentum of the defensive player to pass him as he uses a pushing, sculling motion with his non-passing hand to help him get by. Players with partners take up various positions around the pool to practice this technique.

Variation: The pass can be to a teammate or simply a pass to oneself with a drive to get inside water. Inside water can lead to drive-in shots as well.

Coaching Point:

- This drill is very effective against an overly aggressive, tight man-to-man defense. Players should learn counters for every occasion.

#19 BALL RETURN DRILL

Objective: To improve reactions, anticipation and ball handling skills while providing excellent conditioning.

Description: This drill simulates a game situation where two players go for a loose ball. Two players with one ball perform from three to five series of ten consecutive wet passes at no more than two meters apart. The receiving player must quickly react to the wet pass and return the ball dry to his partner. Return passes should be from the water; quick, firm and dry to the original passer's hand. Passes can be to the side, in front of, or lobbed over the receiver, and should vary so that the receiver cannot anticipate where the next pass will land. Passes need not be more than one or two strokes from the receiver.

Variations: This drill can also be done with groups of three players. One variation features two passers (the ball can be returned to either of the two passers). Another variation uses one passer (two players react to control loose ball when the ball is thrown between them).

Coaching Points:

- This drill is also good for a two-meter player in a situation where the player must save the ball from being stolen and then make a quick release pass.

- This is a quick drill, not more than thirty seconds at a time.

#20 ETERNITY DRILL

Objective: To improve passing and ball handling skills while providing excellent conditioning.

Description: This drill can include from ten to twenty players, two players for each ball. Players form two rows lined up with the goal posts. The first five to ten minutes partners make continuous wet passes while in motion towards one goal, then for the next five to ten minutes they make continuous dry passes while in motion. Each pair is swimming head up in lung pattern, and both must touch the goal posts or end wall, changing sides every two laps. With the lung pattern, after the partners touch the end wall, they circle back to the other end of the pool by swimming outside the inside two rows, continuing to pass from one outside row to the other.

Variations: This drill can be done using only wet passes. Wet inside (short passes) and wet outside (long passes): pick up the ball from underneath and make a lob pass directly in front of partner. Another variation would be to use only dry passes. Dry inside (short passes): dry continuous passing every stroke (timing). The ball must be kept dry. Dry outside (long passes): pick up the ball from underneath and make a direct dry pass to partner. Swim four to five strokes between passes

Coaching Points:

- This drill improves ball awareness and conditioning.

- Insist on good passes as fatigue sets in.

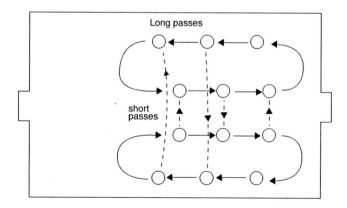

CHAPTER 3

COMBINATION BASIC PASSING DRILLS

INTRODUCTION

CIRCLE DRILLS

The first nine drills in the following chapter are all circle drills that can be used separately, or combined into one continuous series of three-, four-, or five-minute segments. All of the drills are designed to be done right and left handed. Some or all of these drills should be included in the basic warm-up drills during most training sessions.

- Random pass
- Backhand pass
- Cross-face pass
- Spin-and-pass
- "High" hold pass

- Two-hand pass
- Roll and pass
- Two water polo balls
- Tip drill

#21 WARM-UP RANDOM PASS DRILL

Objective: To improve passing skills while emphasizing leg conditioning, body balance, communication and "high" water polo.

Description: Five players form a circle. Each drill starts out with random overhead passing. All drills are performed to the right for two minutes and then to the left for two minutes, and both left and right hands are used for the same drill.

Variation: Straight passes to anyone in the circle using any type of pass, including backhand passes, spin-and-pass, pass and hold and pass, drive center roll - and-pass, and tip pass.

Coaching Points:

- This is an excellent warm-up drill.

- Hand up ready to receive ball.

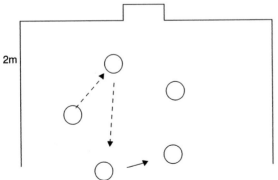

#22 BACKHAND PASS DRILL

Objective: To improve backhand passing skills while emphasizing leg conditioning, body balance, communication and "high" water polo.

Description: Five players form a circle. The ball is passed to the right, caught, and released on the water. Before each pass, players should rotate their right shoulder to the left. Players roll their hand over and under the ball and with their back to the receiver, make a backhanded pass.

Variation: The players may use a dry pass by catching the ball dry, roll hand around and under the ball using wrist action. Players should use their right hands going one direction and their left hands going the other direction.

Coaching Point:

- The coach should constantly check for proper body and shoulder rotations, and high elbow position.

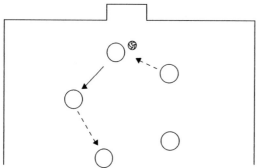

#23 CROSS-FACE PASS DRILL

Objective: To improve cross-face passing skills while emphasizing leg conditioning, body balance, communication and "high" water polo.

Description: Five players form a circle. A right hand, cross-face pass is received by the first player who then rotates to the right until his non-shooting shoulder points toward the next receiver. Non-passing hand and arm must be out of the water and the player must use legs only for turning.

Variation: This same drill using the left hand.

Coaching Point:

- The coach should constantly check on body and shoulder rotations. The player's body position must be correct.

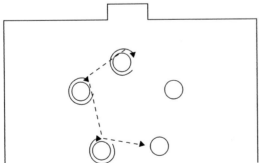

#24 SPIN-AND-PASS DRILL

Objective: To improve player skills in the spin-and-pass technique while emphasizing leg conditioning, body balance, communication and "high" water polo.

Description: Five players form a circle. With the ball going to the right, spin-and-pass right handed. The ball should not be released until the left shoulder points to the receiver. The non-passing hand and arm should be out of the water and the player must use legs only for the turn.

Variation: Same drill using the left hand and going left.

Coaching Points:

- The coach should constantly check on body and shoulder rotation. The player's body position must be correct.

- Non-passing arm's elbow should be significantly high out of the water.

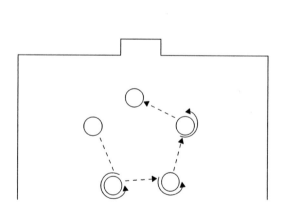

Receive, Spin and Pass
Left shoulder points to next
player before pass

#25 "HIGH" HOLD PASS DRILL

Objective: To improve passing skills while emphasizing leg conditioning, body balance, communication and "high" water polo.

Description: Five players form a circle. Each passer turns and stays "high" in the water, lifting the ball over their head in a throwing motion, shoulder pointing toward receiver. The passer holds in the "high" position for three seconds, and then passes.

Variations: Same drill using the left hand. Drill can also be done like the see-saw drill with each player coming up to receive the ball, then dropping down, then coming up in the water to pass. The ball is caught, released on the water and then picked up with the hand under and passed.

Coaching Points:

- The coach should constantly check on body and shoulder rotations. The player's body position must be correct.

- The players should count out the three seconds.

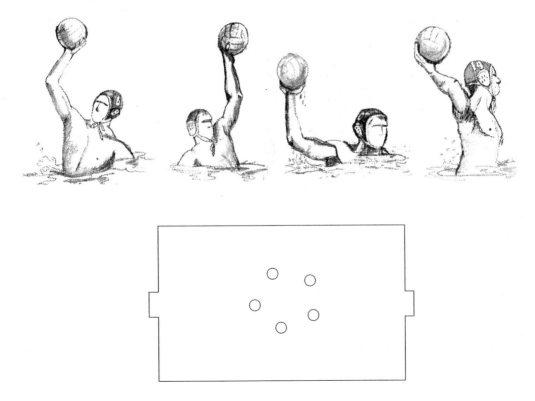

#26 TWO WATER POLO BALLS DRILL

Objective: To improve passing skills while emphasizing leg conditioning, body balance, communication, "high" water polo and peripheral vision.

Description: Five players form a circle. Two balls are passed around the circle, one after the other, with the second ball closely following the first. The passer must be alert to the receiver's readiness. The receiver must be alert to catch the ball, turn, and continue the drill.

Variations: Same drill using the left hand. Non-passing hand and arm should be out of the water and the player must use only his legs for turning. Another variation is to rotate one player into the center, and he passes back and forth to the other players in the circle.

Coaching Points:

- The coach should constantly check on body and shoulder rotations. The player's body position must be correct.

- Each player must be aware of the receiver's readiness to catch the ball.

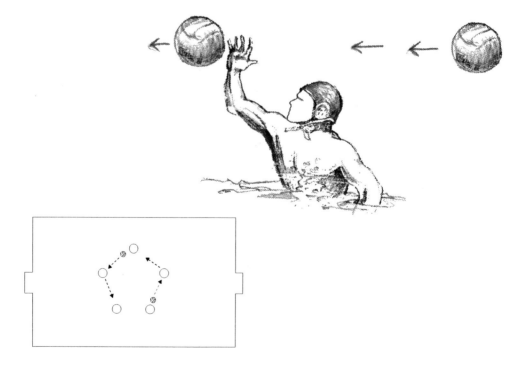

#27 TWO-HAND PASS DRILL

Objective: To improve two-handed passing skills while emphasizing leg conditioning, body balance, communication and "high" water polo.

Description: Five players form a circle. Players pass the ball around the circle using two-handed passes, making sure they bring the ball over and back behind their heads before the pass.

Variation: Same drill performed in the opposite direction.

Coaching Points:

- The coach should constantly check on body and shoulder rotations. The player's body position must be correct.

- Emphasize bringing the ball as far back as possible.

#28 ROLL-AND-PASS DRILL

Objective: To improve skills in rolling while passing, while emphasizing leg conditioning, body balance and communication.

Description: Five players form a wide circle. Each player will dribble the ball to the center of the circle, keeping his body horizontal. Using timing and while continuing the stroke, he must reach under the water and with his hand under the ball, turn and pass back to the next player in the circle.

Variation: Same drill with left hand.

Coaching Points:

- The coach should emphasize that the pass is part of a continuing swimming stroke.

- Players should not be permitted to get into a sitting position as they pass. They must stay horizontal throughout the complete passing sequence.

- Emphasize that the passer sprints back to his original position.

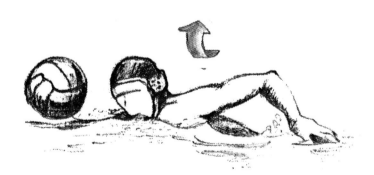

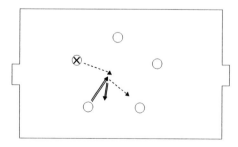

#29 "KEEP THE BALL ALIVE" TIP DRILL

Objective: To improve body balance, body positioning and ball awareness while emphasizing leg conditioning, and "high" water polo.

Description: Five players form a tight circle. The ball is tipped up and all five players attempt to keep the ball in the air. Any player can tip the ball at any time.

Variation: Same drill, only players catch and push the ball up in the air.

Coaching Point:

- In the series of two-meter circle passing drills, this should be the last one.

#30 TWO BALL CENTER PASS DRILL

Objective: To improve passing and ball handling skills as well as ball awareness while moving.

Description: Four players form a box with a fifth player in the center. The center player passes one ball to an outer player, while at the same time, another outer player passes a second ball into the center player. The center player continues to receive and pass the two alternating balls while turning in the center. Substitute for the center player after several rotations.

Variation: This drill should be done with the center player moving both left and right.

Coaching Points:

- The center player must keep both hands up, concentrating on leg and body balance.

- Outer players wait for center player to pass the first ball before passing the second ball into the center.

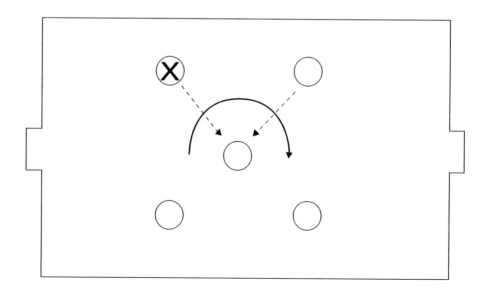

#31 MOBILITY DRILL

Objective: To improve passing and ball handling skills while emphasizing movement and quickness.

Description: Two players face each other four meters apart. Player one passes the ball to player two. After catching the ball, player two quickly turns with the ball, takes two quick strokes, does a quick roll, reaches under the ball and makes an accurate wrist pass to player one. Player one repeats what player two has just done while player two uses big scissors or breaststroke kick to quickly get back to his original position in time to be vertical and ready to catch the next pass.

Variation: Repeat the drill using the other arm.

Coaching Points:

- This drill is simple but important. Put pressure on players by having them count out loud the number of completed passes.

- Intensity drills should be short in duration but done effectively.

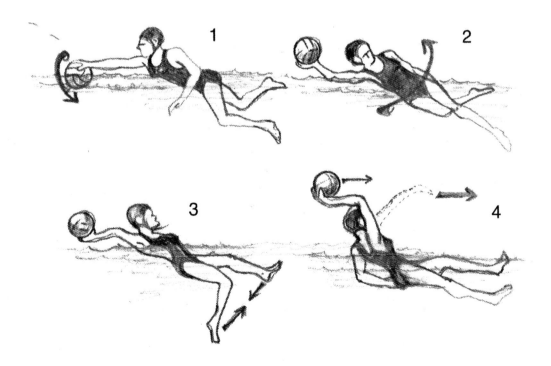

#32 THREE-PLAYER MOBILITY DRILL

Objective: To improve passing skills and ball awareness against a defender.

Description: Two players pass to each other while swimming 25 or 30 meters with a defender between them trying to intercept each pass (keep away). The players rotate into the defender's position.

Variation: The ball may be dribbled and then passed.

Coaching Point:

- This drill is designed to improve ball awareness and passing skills while moving.

#33 QUICK REACTION KEEP AWAY DRILL

Objective: To improve ball awareness, quickness and passing skills under extreme pressure.

Description: This drill involves five players, three on offense and two on defense. Offensive players try to control the ball in an area approximately four meters square, by playing keep away.

Variation: Slightly larger area can be used to accommodate 4-on-3 and 5-on-4, and a smaller area for 2-on-1.

Coaching Points:

- Each drill should be only two or three minutes long, and run in sets of four to six drills.

- This is quite possibly the "best" keep away drill.

- Lane lines should be used to enclose the drill area, or the corners of the pool can be combined with lane lines.

#34 TEAM KEEP-AWAY DRILL

Objective: To improve passing skills, timing and the ability to recognize passing opportunities.

Description: Four to six players on each team, in half court, try to control the ball by playing keep-away. If the defensive team intercepts the ball they go on offense and play keep-away.

Variation: The players are only allowed to hold the ball for three seconds.

Coaching Points:

- This drill trains players in the fundamentals of water polo. The ability to play keep-away is the essence of good water polo, and applies to the front court, counterattack and full scrimmage.

- Players could also run the teams front court offense.

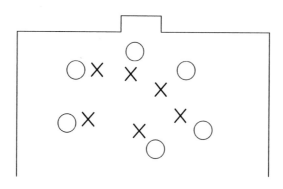

#35 FOUR SQUARE COMBINATION DRILL

Objective: To improve passing and shooting skills while emphasizing coordination and movement.

Description: Players 1, 2 and 3 form a line parallel with goal while player 4 is two meters in front of the goal with the ball. Player 4 passes to player 3 who immediately passes to player 1. Player 2 drives towards the right side of the goal and receives a pass from 1. Player 4 moves across the cage to the opposite side, receives a pass from 2 and shoots.

Variation: Same drill with pass and driver going to the other side.

Coaching points:

- Timing should be such that no player has to wait for the ball to come to him.

- When used as a pre-game warm-up, this drill is often a good indicator of how well the team is concentrating prior to a game.

- Timing is the key – players should be in constant motion with no player waiting for or stopping for a pass.

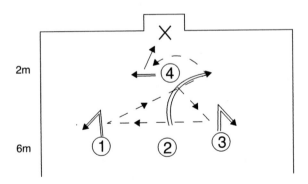

Passing Sequence
4-3-1-2-4

INDIVIDUAL FUNDAMENTALS OF SHOOTING

INTRODUCTION

FUNDAMENTALS OF SHOOTING AND PASSING

Although the rules stipulate that the ball can only be touched by one hand, for proper body positions, all throws should be set-up by bringing both hands into the shooting or passing positions.

The concept behind the value of the two-handed approach is that when both hands reach for the ball, the body follows. Even in a drive shot, the moving of the ball from one hand to the other creates a better opportunity to score by putting the body in its proper alignment.

When coaching the outside shot (five meters or more), even though individual techniques must be accounted for, the fundamental principles of shooting apply. The biomechanics of shooting from the outside are very similar to the baseball pitcher's throw or any long distance baseball throw.

Perhaps the most significant value of the two-handed approach is in the outside shot. The body rotates and turns sideways to the goal as the ball is brought back in a cocked position. Prior to the shot being taken, the elbow is kept high and back, and the ball must be as *far from the head as the high elbow position will allow.*

When reaching for the ball, initially with two hands, the shooting arm goes all the way back into the cocked position, while the non-shooting hand reaches as far as possible, and usually ends up in a line behind the elbow of the shooting arm. This causes the body to turn sideways, with the non-shooting shoulder pointing toward the target. This position is similar to the body mechanics of a baseball pitcher's body. This motion creates better torque, more speed on the ball and a more deceptive shot.

If the description above were freeze-framed, the following would be illustrated:

- The shoulder of the non-shooting arm would be pointing toward the goal.

- The lead leg would be bent with toes pointing toward the goal.

- The back leg would be bent, ready to push backward and down, with the toes pointing sideways (ready to push off).

- The torso is well forward, not backward.

As the ball is in the process of being shot, the back foot turns inward and the *soles of both feel push downward at the same time* – then the hand, arm and body follow through.

In analyzing film taken underwater during shooting drills at the University of California, Berkeley – using 200 frames-per-second film – it was observed that as the ball was released the most accurate shooters were not using the egg-beater kick (which has been advocated for years), but actually *kicked downward with the soles of both feet at the same time.*

The bigger the arm circle, the greater the ball speed. When throwing the ball with full arm motion, it is important that the entire body is used. The torso and shoulder rotate and create maximum torque for power and speed. Wrist action is also extremely important, and should be the first part of the power shot to be emphasized. Simple wrist passing, concentrating on a whip action, or snap translates to good hard speed.

When faking, deception is the key. A fake must make the goalie or defender think the player is shooting or passing. A fake can include any combination of arms, shoulders, chest, hips, and eyes. Faking techniques include the arm only fake, the shoulder and arm combination fake, or the most important, the chest, hip, head combination where everything moves except the ball. This fake is very effective on the power play, (6-on-5) perimeter passing. Shooting practices should include alternating shots from lob to hard, while switching the location of the shots. Players should also practice faking a pass and then shooting, as well as faking a shot and then passing. Always try to use eyes deceptively, however, when necessary look directly into the goalie's eyes rather than the target area. The better the player's ability to show different movements, the easier it is to get the goalie off balance. Players should always work for better angles or to create a better angle for another player. A lob shot should never be the first shot taken in a game. It seems to set the goalie's position better. All lob shots must come off of a fake.

#36 BODY "TORQUE" SHOOTING DRILL

Objective: To improve shooting velocity.

Description: One at a time the players dribble to within six meters of the goal. They bring their knees up under their body while the upper torso rears up into a vertical position. The players pick up the ball and rotate their body with the non-shooting hand almost touching the ball. The players swing their non-shooting arm parallel to the water beginning a torque with their body as the front arm, then chest, shooting arm and ball follow the twisting of the body as the ball is shot. The player's non-shooting arm continues to rotate all the way around until the body is facing sideways. (This action is similar to throwing the discuss in track and field)

Variation: Eventually, the arm action must come over the player's shoulder for proper body mechanics.

Coaching Points:

- This drill is excellent for players who do not have much velocity on the ball when they are passing or shooting the ball. Learning body "torque" significantly increases velocity.

- This is not a proper throwing action, and this drill should be used sparingly on players who need to improve shooting velocity.

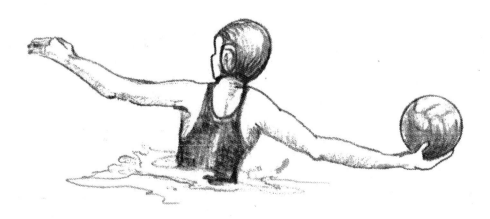

#37 CROSS-FACE PASS AND SHOOT DRILL

Objective: To improve receiving, passing and shooting skills using the cross-face pass.

Description: This drill begins with two lines; one dribbling and the other receiving cross-face passes. The receiving player's body must rotate almost 180 degrees during this exercise. The shooting arm must come in contact with the ball at approximately the outside shoulder of the non-shooting arm. The receiver's body motion should rotate at the same speed as the ball. This rotation permits balance and the ability to shoot at any place in the goal. Leg position as the body rotates is important, and the hip must be up and behind the shoulder line before the shot is attempted.

Variation: This technique can also be practiced as part of a circle passing drill.

Coaching Points:

- The most common error that players make is shooting while they are off balance.

- Emphasize the importance of rotating completely around before shooting the ball.

- Players should come up in the water when shooting.

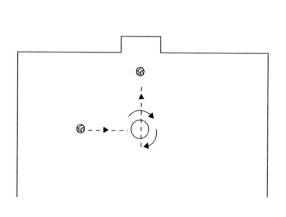

#38 REAR-BACK (RB) SHOOTING DRILL

Objective: To improve shooting skills and release passes using the rear-back (RB) move.

Description: This RB (rear-back) drill begins with the shooter driving in from a position anywhere from half-court to the two-meter line. Using a jackknife body motion — drawing the knees up under the body while the upper torso straightens up — the shooter rears up and back, using the non-shooting arm to help support the body. While rearing up and back, shooter receives a dry pass and shoots. If the shooter is close in and surrounded by defenders, the ball should be caught and released immediately, without bringing the ball all the way back.

Variation: Set up a front court offense with a two-meter player in his position and the other five players in perimeter positions, where they practice release passes back to the two-meter player.

Coaching Points:

- The ball is only brought back behind the shoulder if the situation and time permits.
- Players must stay vertical and not lay on their backs.

#39 BODY ROLL BACKHAND SHOOTING DRILL

Objective: To improve backhand shooting skills while swimming parallel to or away from the goal.

Description: There are two basic techniques for shooting backhand shots. The first requires the players to slide their hand under the ball and roll their body, elbow up, without dropping the ball. In the second, the players reach over and slide their hand under the ball, bringing the ball up so that it rests, if time permits, into their forearm. The shot should be a snap action motion with the elbow high.

Variation: The player may swim across the cage using the shooting arm nearest the goal without stopping the cadence of his stroke. The hand comes under and to the side of the ball and is flicked toward the cage in one fluid motion.

Coaching Points:

- Players should be become proficient with ball handling skills that include right- and left-handed backhand shots while swimming.

- The most common error that players make is shooting while off balance.

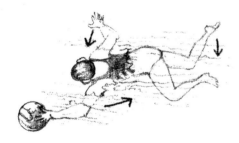 

#40 THE POP-UP SHOT DRILL

Objective: To improve shooting skills using the pop-up shot while swimming.

Description: Players should practice two different methods of the pop-up shot. In the first method, best for surprising the goalie, the player tees up the ball with the non-shooting hand and shoots while swimming a normal crawl stroke. The fingers of the shooting hand come in contact with the ball with the arm and shoulder following through after the ball is shot off the tee. In the second method, the ball is teed up and shot while the player is facing the goal, in a holding position, keeping the guard behind him.

Variation: This shooting technique can also be practiced as part of a circle passing drill.

Coaching Points:

- The shooter's body should ride as high as possible while dribbling and shooting.

- The shooting arm should be completely clear of the water. Turn the palm sideways and away from the center (thumb pointing down).

- Contact with the ball should be with the fingers, not the palm of the hand, driving through the ball towards the goal.

- If close in, and in a holding position, players should draw their knees under their bodies while their arms are cocked to hit the ball.

#41 PUSH SHOT OR PASS DRILL

Objective: To improve shooting and passing skills using one hand while emphasizing quickness.

Description: This technique can be used for drive-ins, shooting, or passing to teammates. While dribbling the ball, the push shot is started by placing one hand on top of the ball and pressing down slightly, then allowing the ball to rise until it is slightly clear of the water. At this point, the shot is executed just as in the pop shot.

Variation: The player may bring the ball toward his shoulder with his thumb under the ball and palm against the ball.

Coaching Points:

- Players should approach the ball with both hands

- When the defender is on one side of the shooter, the shooter can use his free arm to continue stroking as he shoots with his other arm.

- Emphasize that players should concentrate on bringing their knees up to the chest and extending as they shoot.

#42 CROSSOVER BACKHAND SHOT DRILL

Objective: To improve backhand shooting skills.

Description: Players should perfect two different arm motions when practicing crossover backhand shots. In the first method the ball is shot with a simple flick of the wrist while keeping the arm straight. The elbow remains straight and is turned toward the target. The advantages to this method include a quick release and short-range accuracy.

The second method is the bent arm backhand. This spectacular shot produces great velocity, but is more difficult to control. Leg motion is very important in this technique, and they should be drawn up under the chest and then extended when the ball is shot.

Variation: These methods can also be practiced as part of a circle passing drill.

Coaching Points:

- The most common error that players make is shooting the ball while off balance.

- Emphasize to players they should rotate completely around and draw their legs under their bodies before shooting.

- Players can practice different shots by driving in from different angles.

#43 SCREW SHOT DRILL

Objective: To improve shooting and passing skills while driving using the screw shot or pass.

Description: The shot should begin with the non-shooting hand assisting with the pick up. The player places the shooting hand under the ball and supports the ball just clear of the water. As the arm is drawn back to the shooting position, the shoulders and body rotate. The arm is drawn back to the shoulder release position and then shoots forward in a piston-like motion. From under the ball, the player's hand rotates over the ball. The thumb rotates below the ball (pointing to the bottom of the pool). The player's hand is twisted under the ball, causing the elbow to be high. Leg position is again important, and the player should draw the knees up toward the chest and then extend the legs as the ball is shot.

Variation: This can be a circle passing drill or a drive-in shooting drill.

Coaching points:

- The most common error that players make is shooting while off balance.
- While this is not a power shot, there will be less velocity on the ball if the shooter's legs are not brought up and then extended when the shot is made.

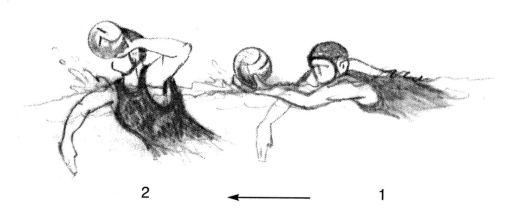

2   ←   1

#44 TETHERBALL DRILL

Objective: To improve shooting skills by increasing arm strength and duplicating throwing motion against resistance.

Description: Attach a tetherball to a wall using flexible surgical tubing. Players practice throwing motions with resistance. Beginning with the basic throw, the player places throwing hand under the ball with the tubing between the fingers. Exercise can be done in segments, i.e., from when the ball is all the way back to just moving it to shoulder level. Then they can work on motion from shoulder to release point, to the complete follow-through.

Variations: Various throwing/shooting motions should be practiced including the two-hand, where the players pull the ball down in a forward movement from behind the head, and the backhand, in which the players face the ball and place their hand under the ball. They should then perform the spin and scoop shot movement with their back to the ball. Sets of 20, repeating as desired.

Coaching Points:

- This drill is used prior to entry into the water.

- This can be a gradual warm-up before players use a regulation ball.

- When a full arm action is used, the position of the legs is important. At the beginning of the throw, the lead foot points forward and the back leg is bent with the foot pushing down.

#45 OUTSIDE SHOOTING DRILL

Objective: To improve shooting skills from the outside while emphasizing proper body rotation.

Description: The player picks up the ball, turns sideways while rotating back, and brings the ball back (not close to the player's head). The player's elbow should be above the shoulder as the elbow leads in bringing the ball over shoulder. There should be acceleration through the throw. The position of the legs is identical to a baseball pitcher, with the front leg bent at the knee, toes pointing toward the goal, and the back leg bent down, with toes pointed to the side. As the ball is shot, the back foot turns inward and then both feet kick back and down at the same time.

Variation: This shooting drill can begin by using a dribble, picking up the ball or receiving a pass.

Coaching Points:

- The longer the wind-up the more effective and deceptive the shot and the better the opportunity to score.

- Do not allow body to rock backwards.

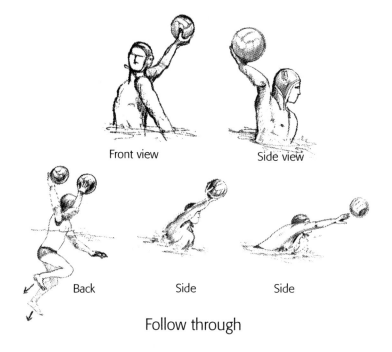

Front view   Side view

Back   Side   Side

Follow through

#46 MEDICINE BALL PASSING DRILL

Objective: To improve shooting and passing skills by increasing arm strength through training with a heavy object.

Description: After weight training and prior to entering the water to practice passing, players make two-handed passes using a two-to-four kilo medicine ball. In the water, with one hand, groups of three players pass the medicine ball while at least a meter apart. As the players become adept at using the weighted ball, add a real water polo ball so that they can adjust to the different weight.

Coaching Points:

- This exercise should be closely supervised.

- Keep passes short from one to four meters.

- After the medicine ball drill, have a long warm-up with regulation water polo ball, practicing short and long passes and shots.

#47 TURN AND SHOOT DRILL

Objective: To improve shooting skills using the turn and shoot while being guarded.

Description: The two-meter player pushes firmly with his back against the guard's chest, then reaches under the ball, turns and shoots the ball. Players can line up in pairs in two rows approximately four meters apart and practice this shot back and forth to each other.

Variation: Drill should be practiced using both hands.

Coaching Points:

- The two-meter shooters do NOT overtly push off the defender; they just lean with their back, not their head. Avoid offensive fouls.

- Shooter does not move away from established position.

- Players may practice in pairs in a line formation, however, the most effective drill is with a goal and goalie.

- This is an effective drill for receiving and protecting the ball in the front court offense.

#48 THE STEP-OUT DRILL

Objective: To improve shooting skills using a step-out shot while being guarded

Description: The two-meter player pushes his back firmly against the guard's chest, moves parallel to the guard, then reaches under the ball, turns and with lead foot "stepping out", pivots around that leg, turns and shoots the ball.

Variation: A right-hander can step out and cross over his own right shoulder and shoot.

Coaching Points:

- The two-meter shooters do NOT overtly push off the defender, they lean with their back, not their head.

- Players may practice in pairs in a line formation, however, the most effective drill is with a goal and goalie.

#49 LAYOUT DRILL

Objective: To improve shooting skills using a layout shot while being guarded.

Description: Player's hips must be high. Bringing the knees under the body, players use a scissors or breaststroke kick to roll onto their back and place their shooting hand under the ball, then shoot down the length of their body.

Variations: One form of this drill requires the player to roll and shoot in one fluid motion. Another, is to have the player roll on his back and kick using scissors, breaststroke or flutter, to gain separation from the guard.

Coaching Points:

- Players should layout and press shoulders back in the water. There is a tendency to roll up in a rocking chair position, which inhibits the velocity of the shot.

- Players may practice in pairs in a line formation, however, the most effective drill is with a goal and goalie.

- Pick-up ball from bottom – cradle the ball, don't grab for it.

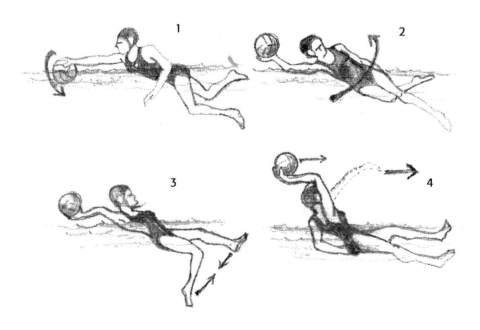

#50 WRIST OVER SHOULDER SHOOTING DRILL

Objective: To improve shooting skills when a guard over plays the power side of the shooter by using a wrist-over-shoulder shot.

Description: When the guard over-plays the power side of the two-meter player (turning side), the two-meter player should keep his back pressed against the guard. The two-meter player reaches under the ball, palm up with his thumb pointing to the opposite shoulder and, rotating his wrist parallel to the water, flicks the ball to the opposite corner of the goal.

Variation: This guard position also sets up the backhand shot.

Coaching Points:

- The players should be reminded to constantly be aware of the guard's position since that will dictate the type of shot to be used.

- Working with a goal and goalie is the most effective way to practice this drill.

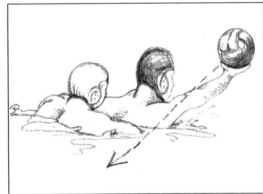

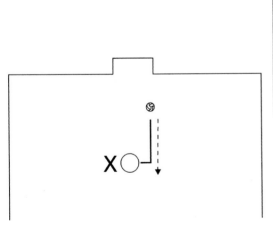

#50 SPIN OR SCOOP SHOT DRILL

Objective: To improve shooting skills using a spin or scoop shot while being guarded.

Description: The two-meter player begins with his back to the cage and the defender. He brings his legs under his body in a scissors or breaststroke position. Reaching under the ball with the shooting hand, the player's body uncoils, spins and swings the shooting arm to shoot. Player should keep the arm straight and parallel to the water during the shot.

Variations: This drill should be practiced both right- and left-handed. Another method is to use the wrist without the body whip. The player may also use leverage against the guard, slide sideways and then shoot the ball.

Coaching Points:

- To create cross-cage shots, shooter must keep his hand on the ball longer.
- All variations should be practiced by the two-meter players and, depending on the position of the guard, they must be able to employ the various moves.
- Working with just the goal, and then later adding the goalie and a defender is the most effective way to practice this drill.
- Two-meter players who do not have a strong eggbeater kick can use the scissor kick effectively to create the "uncoiling" of the body, and produce the whipping action as the shot follows.
- This shot resembles the technique used by a discus thrower. As with all throws that begin in the water, use both hands, alternately, to set up the sweep. The ball is thrown with a straight arm, low and parallel to the surface of the water. As the ball is released, the body action of the head, shoulders, hips and final thrust of the legs creates the velocity.

#52 DEFLECTION SHOT DRILL

Objective: To practice the deflection shot to surprise the goalie and guard.

Description: After communication, a player actually shoots toward the two-meter player attempting to get the ball within arms length in front of him. The two-meter player uses the back of his hand to deflect the ball over his shoulder, and past the defenders.

Variation: Tip shots from dry passes.

Coaching Point:

- This is a very chancy — perhaps last second of a quarter — desperation shot. The players must have excellent communication between the passer and the two-meter player in order for this play to be successful.

CHAPTER 5

SHOOTING DRILLS

#53 TWENTY SHOTS FROM TWO-METER LINE DRILL

Objective: To improve shooting and ball handling skills while emphasizing conditioning and intensity.

Description: This drill involves rapid passing. The player at the two-meter line will catch the ball being passed from the opposite post, coming up as high as possible and then shooting directly down into the corner of the cage. The passer should not delay the next pass. Other players feed the passer to eliminate any delay.

Variations: Using the backhand on one corner, players shoot straight down on the near corner (depending if right- or left-handed). The second rotation could include everyone shooting right-handed or left-handed.

Coaching Point:

- Coaches should make this a motivation drill by encouraging the players to come up high and shoot down hard onto the water.

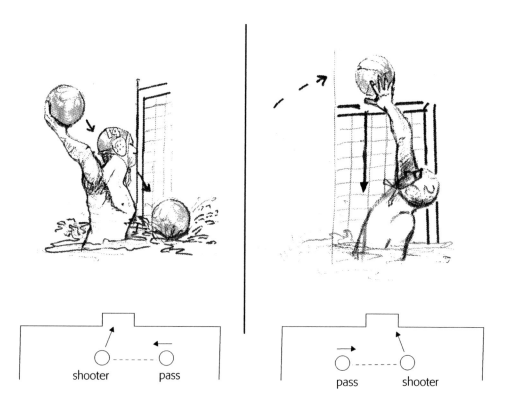

shooter   pass

pass   shooter

#54 TWENTY SHOTS FROM SIX-METER LINE DRILL

Objective: To improve shooting and ball handling skills while emphasizing conditioning and intensity.

Description: This drill requires rapid passing from the wing to the players at the six-meter line who must catch and shoot without faking. The passer should not delay the pass. The other players feed the passer to eliminate delay. If the pass is overthrown or dropped, it is ignored and the passing continues.

Variations: The pass comes from the other side. Shots can be taken in line with the right post and the left post for an additional drill.

Coaching Point:

- Coaches should make this a motivational drill by encouraging the players to shoot as rapidly as possible.

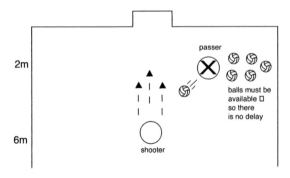

#55 TWENTY-FIVE OR THIRTY METER INTENSITY DRIVE-IN DRILL

Objective: To increase intensity and aggressiveness when a player has the offensive advantage.

Description: The offensive player starts with a lead and is chased a full 25 or 30 meters, receiving the ball at the halfway point. If the offensive player is caught, he holds the defensive player by positioning and staying with inside water. The defensive player tries to get inside position without fouling.

Variation: A pass is thrown from the offensive goalie position so that when the offensive player rolls on his back for three strokes and calls for the ball, the goalie makes a wet pass in front of the offensive player.

Coaching Point:

- Emphasize that the offensive player holds his position and does not hook out.

#56 MOMENTUM SHOOTING DRILL WITH PASS FROM BACKCOURT

Objective: To improve shooting skills while emphasizing intensity, movement and momentum.

Description: In the basic center drive drill, the player sprints towards the goal, rolls onto his back, rears up to receive the pass at about six or seven meters, turns and shoots the ball.

Variations: Same drill with the player catching and shooting from around two meters. Drill can also be done with passes to either side, and using either hand. Also, shooter can use backhand, guide or tip shots. Two-meter shots should be practiced without a goalie. This can include tipping or directing the ball.

Coaching Points:

- In the basic drill, emphasize that the players look down at the goal when shooting. This is an excellent pre-game warm-up drill.

- Emphasize leg position, balance and timing to receive the ball.

#57 FOUR MINUTE SHOOTING DRILLS
A. QUICK DRIVE-IN SHOTS

Objective: To take as many shots as possible in four minutes.

Description: Begin with five or six players at each goal, without a goalie. The players practice dribbling drive-in shots for four minutes from the center. The coach starts his watch and the players take shots as rapidly as possible .

Variation: Practice the same four-minute drill while driving in from both wings.

Coaching Points:

- The coach can add an element of competition to this drill by establishing a scoring system; for each goal, a point is earned. The four-minute drills should account for about 45-60 minutes of shooting.

- Players retrieve their own shot.

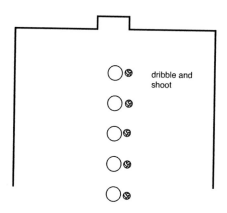

dribble and shoot

#57 FOUR MINUTE SHOOTING DRILLS
B. RIGHT ANGLE SHOTS

Objective: To take as many shots as possible in four minutes.

Description: Begin with five or six players at each goal without a goalie. The players dribble to the three-meter line, turn right and swim parallel to the goal. If a right-hander is shooting, she shoots a quick wrist release to left corner. If left-handed, he uses a backhand shot into the left corner.

Variations: Same drill only to the opposite side with right- and left-handers flip-flopping shots. This drill can be also run using backhand shots.

Coaching Points:

- The coach can make this a contest by establishing a scoring system; for each goal, a point is earned. The four-minute drills should account for about 45-60 minutes of shooting.

- Body must be parallel to the goal.

#57 FOUR MINUTE SHOOTING DRILLS
C. CLOCKWISE/COUNTER CLOCKWISE CATCH AND SHOOT

Objective: To take as many shots as possible in four minutes.

Description: Begin with five or six players at each goal without a goalie. The players drive to three meters, receive a pass from the right wing and shoot. The right-handed players catch and shoot anywhere in goal. If left-handed, they catch and shoot cross-face.

Variations: The same drill should be performed to the opposite side with the left- and right-handers flip-flopping shots. Another variation would have the players tipping or guiding the ball in.

Coaching Points:

- The coach can make this a contest; points are earned for each successful shot. This drill should be part of a 45 to 60 minute passing and shooting practice segment.

- Encourage cross-cage shots.

- No goalie is used from the three meter distance.

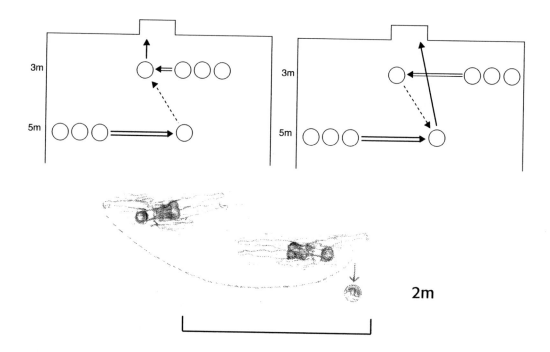

#57 FOUR MINUTE SHOOTING DRILLS
D. CROSSING, PASSING AND SHOOTING

Objective: To take as many shots a possible in four minutes.

Description: Begin with five or six players at each goal without a goalie. Two lines of players, one on each side of the goal. Players in the line on the left, closest to the goal, are the shooters. The line on the right are dribblers and passers. First players in both lines start swimming across the middle at the same time. Player from the right side dribbles across, rolls to pass back to the right side of shooter who rolls on his back and shoots without stopping. Then the shooter goes to the passing line and the passer to the shooting line.

Variations: Run the same drill with dribblers closest to the goal and the shooters outside. Also, switch sides so shooting from both directions.

Coaching Point:

- The coach can make this drill a contest; points are earned for each successful shot.

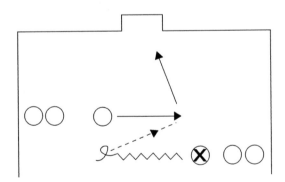

#58 ACCURACY AND CONTROL SHOOTING DRILL

Objective: To improve shooting accuracy while emphasizing conditioning.

Description: The players shoot from various distances and attempt to hit the net without hitting the bar or the water.

Variation: Allow the players to shoot wet shots as well.

Coaching Points:

- This drill is designed to get players to understand the concept of shooting through the net, and help develop control and accuracy.

- The coach can mandate that the loosing players (or the group) be required to do ten push-ups or swim twenty-five or thirty meter butterfly if a bar is hit or the goal is missed.

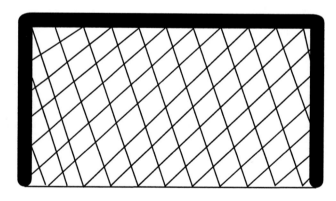

#59 DRIVE-IN SHOOTING DRILL

Objective: To improve inside water drives and drive-in shots while being defended.

Description: The offensive player with the ball dribbles away from the goal and at the opportune time, reverses direction and goes for a drive-in shot with the defender chasing and/or stopping the shot.

Variation: The guard alternates being on the right and left side of the offensive player.

Coaching Points:

- Call four-meter fouls. Encourage defenders to try and get position without causing an ejection foul or four-meter violation.

- The offensive player must go for the shot, not the penalty.

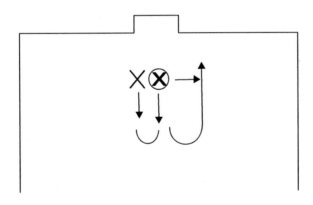

#60 PARALLEL PASS BACK AND SHOOT DRILL

Objective: To improve shooting and ball handling skills while emphasizing body balance.

Description: Players form two lines. The dribbler swims to approximately six meters, picks up the ball and passes it to his teammate who is parallel. The teammate then passes it back and the shot is taken.

Variations: Run the same drill using three or four passes. Drill can also be performed with the dribbler starting from the opposite side.

Coaching Points:

- The coach should emphasize starting quickly, passing and receiving direct passes and shooting a quick shot.

- Each player, even when not shooting, must still rotate and get their body into shooting position – thereby making the goalie commit.

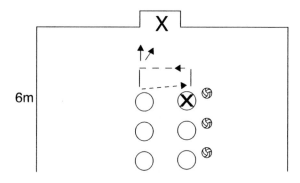

#61 TIMING REAR-BACK (RB) SHOOTING DRILL

Objective: To improve shooting and passing skills while emphasizing coordination and timing.

Description: Players form two lines. First player from line one, dribbles while sprinting up to the two-meter line, where he turns and throws, in one motion, back to the first player in line two, who is positioning himself center cage at about the five-meter line. Without slowing down, player two catches and shoots.

Variation: This drill should be performed from the other side as well.

Coaching Point:

- This drill is designed to encourage timing, with no waiting for the pass or shot. Players should be able to key off of one another, which is the purpose of this drill.

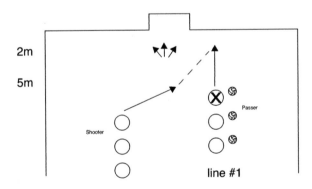

#62 TANDEM SHOOTING DRILL

Objective: To improve ball handling skills while emphasizing the importance of movement to open up situations.

Description: Two players, swimming side-by-side, start ten meters from the goal. They move together in the same formation, then one player passes to the other player who shoots the ball.

Variation: Put a defender between the offensive tandem

Coaching Point:

- The pair should start and end slightly outside the right and left goal posts.

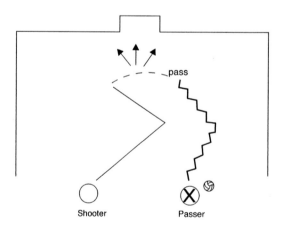

#63 THREE-SHOT DRILL

Objective: To improve directional shooting skills while emphasizing movement and body balance.

Description: Three passers line up in a row. Passer A is on the three-meter line, passer B is on the six-meter line and passer C is on the nine-meter line. The shooter makes a hooking move on the nine-meter line, receives the ball from passer A, and shoots a skip shot to the lower left corner. Then the shooter after hooking again at the six-meter line, receives a second ball this time from passer B, and shoots cross-cage high or low. Then, after going directly to the two-meter line, the shooter receives a pass from passer C, and shoots down on water near the left post.

Variation: Run the drill from left side using the same shooting directions.

Coaching Points:

- Emphasize the hooking action.

- On the last pass, the shooter should come up high in the water and shoot down with as much force as possible.

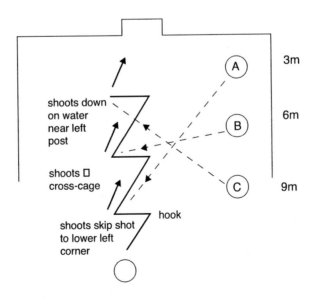

#64 TWO-ON-TWO WITH PASSER DRILL

Objective: To improve RB moves for releases and/or shots while emphasizing beating the defender for drive-in shots.

Description: On the coach's whistle this drill begins with the two-meter picking up the ball and passing to one of two players at about the six-meter line. They are attempting to free themselves from their defenders for an RB, a shot, a release to each other, a release back to the two-meter player or a drive-in shot.

Variations: This drill can be performed from each wing as well as the center. Using drive-in shots make the drill more game-like for the offense and defense.

Coaching Point:

- The coach can use his whistle more to encourage the players to keep moving. After each shot, the coach resets the situation.

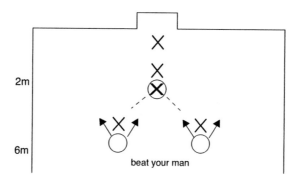

CHAPTER 6

COUNTERATTACK DRILLS

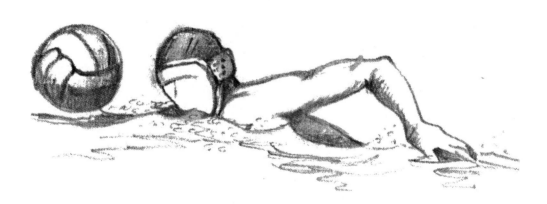

INTRODUCTION

THE COUNTERATTACK

Considered the most exciting phase of the game of water polo, the counterattack requires quickness, speed and endurance. Even when there is no numerical advantage, the counterattack gets players into their offensive front court positions quicker, and it forces the opponent to work harder to get their offense going. A good counterattack system becomes a defensive tactic too, since it forces the opponents to consistently get back on their own defensive end of the court.

The two basic ways to get the ball down the court as quickly as possible, are the long pass (which is the most desirable because the defense cannot get set), and the half-court wing (which allows lead break to get to the two-meter line). In a 25-meter course, the long pass is the most desired method, and has basically become the rule. Another general rule is that successful counterattacks should take three passes or less.

What should be emphasized to the players is that they must get free from their defender in order to advance the ball to the teammate who has the best opportunity to score. One key to a successful counterattack is the goalie. Their vision, ball control, passing ability, and in many occasions ability to institute the attack properly, can determine whether the counterattack is successful or not.

The lead break method means that two players drive to the two-meter line on the right and left side of the opponent's goal, getting there as soon as possible. The second pair of players, back at approximately half court, are the "half-court wings." These wings must be adept at making hard right-angle hooks in order to be free to receive and advance the ball quickly.

One caution on the counterattack: ball control is vital, because the team will be vulnerable to a counter off of their counter. Another rule is to only commit one offensive player more than the defense has back. In case the shot is missed, the counterattacking players must anticipate their defensive positions. The shooter on a counterattack must be aware of his teammates defensive positions before the shot is taken. This is particularly true with a shot from six meters or more. When a counterattack shot is taken, the offensive team is most vulnerable.

A list of additional counterattack principles includes:

- Know the formations, or spots, to which the players must swim in order to have the best opportunity to score.

- Counter rotations are very effective.

- The fewer the number of passes, the more effective the counter-attack.

- Consider a six-on-five counter as either a 3-3 or a 4-2 set-up.

- A second pass counter is good for ball control, as it specifically aids in bringing up the whole team, but the long pass counter is the most successful.

- The most effective fast break is to get the ball down the pool on the goalie's right side – unless the team is made up of primarily left-handed players.

- To holdup on a counter, the goalie should pass the ball cross-court toward the left side of the field of play. (However, a 3-on-2 counter may be effective.)

- If the lead break does not get the ball, the third player receiving the ball goes to the point that creates the triangle.

#65 HESITATION DRIVE DRILL

Objective: To improve driving skills by getting the defender off balance.

Description: The player keeps the defender backing up by starting and stopping, i.e., starting left then going right. Driver works to get the defender into a vertical position so he can swim by.

Variations: Drill can include a pass from the wing. Another variation is to have the offensive player swim by and roll sideways, lifting the arm nearest the defender up and away. At the same time, the arm away from the defender goes deeper underwater, possibly against the defender's hip. Practice with alternate hands.

Coaching Points:

- The driver should begin by moving slowly toward the defensive player, starting just outside of his arms reach, then drive to one side.

- Once past the defender, the driver must accelerate his speed.

#66 DRIVE-IN FACE-TO-FACE MOVEMENT

Objective: To improve driving skills by using the spin and drive-in to get inside water or to continue an offensive drive.

Description: The offensive player moves forward toward the defensive player until they are face-to-face (sometimes the defender will hold the offensive player). The driver positions his face as close as possible to the defender. The offensive player turns very slowly (spins) until parallel or inside, then continues to drive-in.

Variation: Practice this move from all positions on the perimeter of the front court, using both left and right spins.

Coaching Points:

- The smoother the move, the less chance for an offensive foul (no splash).
- This movement is effective for two-meter players as well.

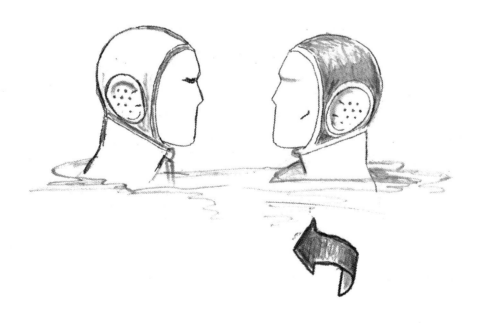

#67 THREE-ON-TWO COUNTERATTACK DRILL

Objective: To practice setting up in proper formation for a three-on-two attack.

Descriptions: Two lead break players drive to the two-meter line and two defenders drop back with them. The coach's whistle starts the center player with the ball. The player with the ball picks up the ball two meters from any defender. If any defensive player switches position, the center player passes to the open teammate, otherwise he shoots the ball.

Variations: Add a defensive player to chase the center player. In a 25- or 30-meter course, set up a counter. Make defenders counterattack on the shot.

Coaches Points:

- This effective counter must be mastered by the players. Each drill should be performed at maximum effort and concentration.

- The fewer the number of passes, the better this works.

- No shots should be taken until the triangle is set.

#68 TWO-PLAYER BREAKAWAY WITH DEFENDERS CHASING DRILL

Objective: To improve breakaway skills, including the goalie's ability to identify the open player and the player's ability to receive the ball under pressure and continue to an offensive shot attempt.

Description: Two offensive players are positioned on the outside of two chasing defenders. They drive toward the two-meter line, and once they get past half court, the goalie passes to the player with the best advantage over his defender. Upon receiving the pass, the player continues toward the goal and attempts a shot.

Variation: Counter the counter. As the shot is taken, or the ball is intercepted, the defenders go on offense and the drill is repeated in the opposite direction.

Coaches Point:

- The goalie's first look and best opportunity, if both players are evenly guarded, is to pass to the right.

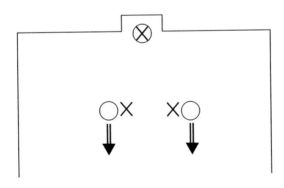

#69 COUNTERATTACK FORMATIONS DRILL

Objective: To improve the player's ability to identify, with communication, all the extra-player formations.

Description: No defenders are used in this drill. Six field players congregate in random positions around mid-pool. A goalie with extra water polo balls is in each goal. The players start with a one-on-goalie, where one player breaks toward the goal while another takes a wing and passes down to the breakaway player. All of the other players must call out the situation. Practice alternates from goal to goal until a six-on-five attack is set. The shot should not be taken until the formation is set.

The formations: *One-on-goalie* — player gets to the five-meter line for the shot. *Two-on-one* — players are one meter wide of the goal posts on the three-meter line. *Three-on-two* — players are slightly behind the two-meter line, one and a half meters outside the goal posts. The third player is on the five- or six-meter line. *Four-on-three* — two players slightly behind the two-meter line, one and a half meters wide of the goal posts, with two players on the six-meter line. *Five-on-four* — three players are across and in front of the cage, slightly behind the two-meter line and two players are on the six-meter line. *Six-on-five* — on the two-meter line (slightly behind) four players take up the following positions: one on each post, two at one and a half meters outside of the post and two on the six-meter line. For a quick set-up use a 3-3 formation.

Variations: Drill is done using only dry passes. Another variation is to run the drill up to the six-on-five formation, and then back down to one-on-goalie formation.

Coaching Points:

- Every player must communicate the formations. These formations must be ingrained into each players mind so they react instinctively.

- In a counterattack, only one player more than the number of defenders is necessary. This helps to protect against a defensive counterattack.

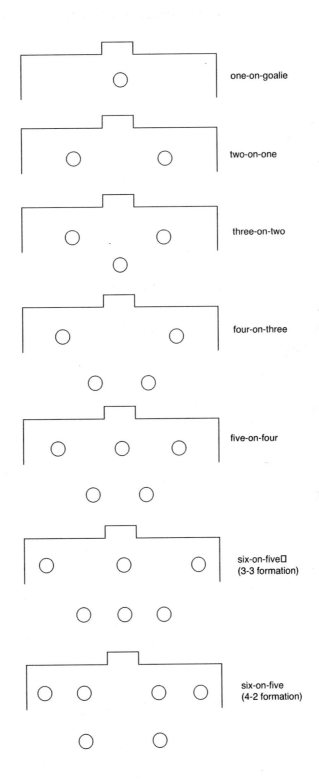

one-on-goalie

two-on-one

three-on-two

four-on-three

five-on-four

six-on-five
(3-3 formation)

six-on-five
(4-2 formation)

#70 FULL-COURT COUNTERATTACK OFF THE SHOOTER DRILL

Objective: To practice anticipating a counterattack when playing defense.

Description: As the offensive player shoots, the defender on the inside fakes blocking the shot and then continues down the court with the offensive shooter chasing. The defender-turned-driver will get a pass from either the goalie or a designated passer.

Variations: Repeat this drill from the other end of the pool. The defender can be positioned on the outside of the shooter and run the counter with an outside release.

Coaches Points:

- The offensive player should always be distracted, even if the guard can not get there to block the shot.

- The concept of this drill is that whatever happens, the defender is always thinking about a counter reaction.

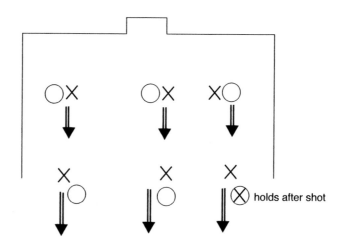

#71 RIGHT-ANGLE WING PASS TO DRIVER DRILL

Objective: To improve counterattack skills, including the goalie's ability to identify the open player and the player's ability to receive the ball and pass to the other wing.

Description: The two offensive players counter down the pool. The player on the right makes a right-angle hook, receives the ball from the goalie and passes quickly to the other player breaking down the left side.

Variation: The same drill is repeated on the other side.

Coaches Point:

- After the players have mastered the techniques in this drill, the coach may add the first defender, chasing on the left, then add a second defender on the half-court wing on the right.

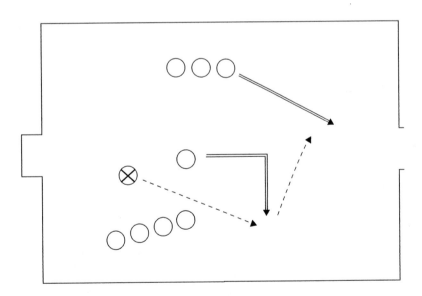

#72 SEQUENTIAL WINGS DRILL

Objective: To practice getting all the players into the front court and taking the ball deep into the opponent's end using constant motion and proper timing.

Descriptions: The goalie passes to half court as player one drives toward the center then hooks out to receive the pass. When player one hooks out, player two, further down the court, drives to the center then hooks out to receive a pass from player one. The same timing works for player three, who drives to the two-meter line. Player three hooks out and receives player two's pass.

Variation: Alternately practice on both sides of pool. Wings make hard right-angle drives after starting toward the center.

Coaches Points:

- This maneuver is very effective because when the ball is received at the two-meter line it is easier to anticipate the counter from that position. The transition and front court offense is immediately set.

- The timing of the passes should be such that no player waits for the ball.

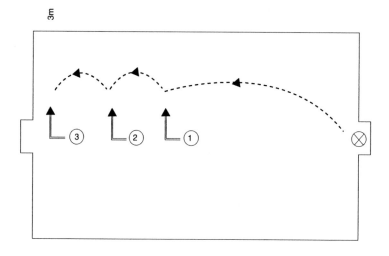

#73 SECOND PASS COUNTERATTACK SYSTEM DRILL

Objective: To practice getting a lead break to the two-meter area while having the center player drive to the ball side.

Description: Three offensive players are involved in this attack. Player two drives down and hooks out just outside the two-meter line. Player one makes a wing at half court. Player three must get to the ball side as he drives the center. The goalie passes to player one, who passes to player two, who then passes to player three. Player three, with a defensive man on him, drives for inside, ball-side water.

Variation: Add defenders to player two and player one.

Coaches Point:

- For this counter to be consistent, center driver MUST get to the ball side.

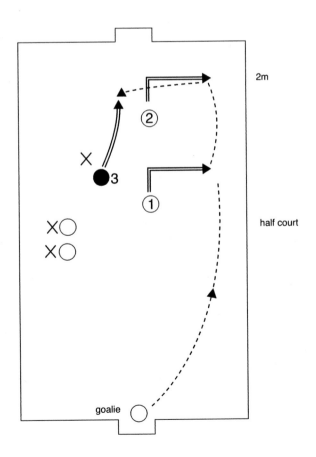

#74 COUNTERATTACK PROGRESSIONS DRILL

Objective: To improve counterattacks by developing combination drills that set up a progression of plays.

Description: Begin with a basic drive-in shot with just a shooter and a goalie. Then add a defensive player chasing. Next, add another defender at two meters and an offensive player, also at two meters – using a counter rotation. Finally add one more offensive player in the center at two meters, who has the option of popping out while the other two-meter offensive player stays behind the line of the ball.

Variation: Run this drill from both sides.

Coaching Point:

- Progressions help players of all skill levels develop a better under-standing of the game.

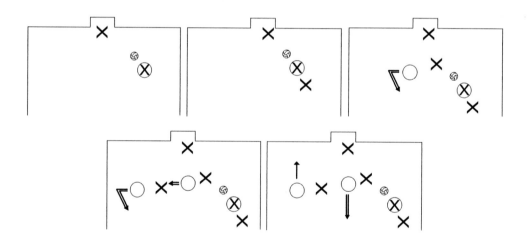

#75 COUNTER ROTATIONS DRILL

Objective: To improve driving skills while emphasizing recognition of driving opportunities with proper rotations and timing.

Descriptions: Player one has the ball and drives towards the goal. If the goalie commits to the driver, he passes to player two, who moves across the cage and slightly back into a passing lane. If the goalie commits to player two, player one shoots the drive-in. Players must always be aware of the goalie's position.

Variations: The coach may add an offensive player, but player three moves parallel and back. Then player two moves to player three's position. Defensive players can then be added with a chaser on player one and defender on two and three. This drill should also be practiced on the opposite side.

Coaching Point:

- Proper timing and the ability to make themselves available for the pass are critical skills for players two and three. They must move at the right time in order to give the driver the opportunity to make the goalie commit. If this is done in tandem, it becomes more successful.

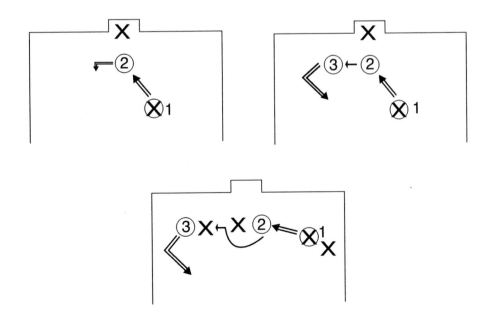

#76 SIX-PLAYER COUNTERATTACK DRILL

Objective: To practice a six-player counterattack while forcing the opponent's two-meter player (or other players who are deep into your half court) to swim down and play defense.

Descriptions: Six players line up in pairs. Two players on the two-meter line, two on the four-meter line and two on the six-meter line. The six-meter players swim to the two-meter line. The four-meter players make a mid-pool hook, and the two-meter players counter out of backcourt toward the two-meter line.

Variations: The goalie may pass to either half-court wing, who then advances the ball to the deep wing, who will pass to players driving down the center. Center players can screen off of each other. Another variation is for the pass to be handled by every player. Passing the opposite way is for another variation.

Coaching Points:

- This drill will help with timing so that no player has to wait for the ball. The key is constant motion.

- This drill is designed to force the opponent's two-meter player and offensive players to commit to defense. It also makes it more difficult for their offensive players to get back to their offensive positions.

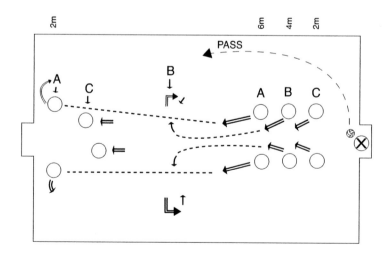

#77 COUNTERATTACK OUT FROM FIVE-ON-SIX DRILL

Objective: To improve transition from being a player down to counterattacking.

Descriptions: Begin the drill with the offense in a 4-2 extra player formation. The defense is set in a 3-2 zone. On the coach's whistle, an offensive player shoots the ball. The defense counters out, with the top player countering strong-side and making a sharp hook to get his defender to follow him. Player two, from the center position, drives along with player three. This creates a 2-on-1 in front of the goal.

Variation: Counter out to the opposite side. (Not as effective)

Coaches Points:

- This is a desperation play to be used when a goal attempt is absolutely necessary, because pulling the center player out leaves the goal unguarded.

- The goalie should have an extra ball in order to facilitate a quick pass if the ball that was shot is not available.

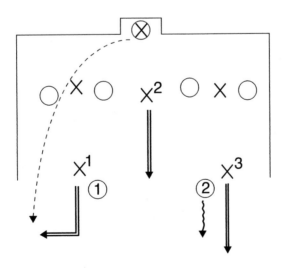

#78 CONTROLLED FULL COURT DRILL

Objective: To improve player's ability to recognize, read and create counterattack situations.

Description: The teams line up in a 3-3 formation with six defenders. The positions remain static. The offensive players pass the ball to each other without interference from the defensive players. When the whistle is blown, the player holding the ball shoots, and then holds for three seconds before he chases the counterattack. The five defensive players attempt to stop the attack.

Variation: Once the team gets to the opposite end, the defensive team becomes the offensive team. Counter the counter — whether a goal is scored or not, (or if they score, they stay on the offense). This will force the counterattack team to recognize the defense as well.

Coaching Points:

- Emphasis should be made on outside shooting. The whistle can be blown in the back or front court to create counterattack situations, such as three-on-two with a chaser. This makes the two-meter player chase.

- The coach can set a variety of extra player situations.

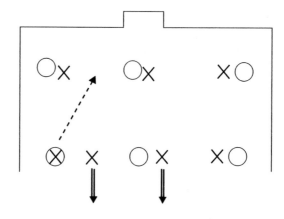

CHAPTER 7

TWO-METER PLAYER
AND
FRONT COURT OFFENSE

INTRODUCTION

FRONT COURT OFFENSE AND TWO-METER PLAYER

Front court offense starts with the transition from defense to offense, from counterattack to ball control. When the transition and the counterattack ends, the front court offense begins. In today's game, front court offense revolves around the two-meter player. This player is closest to the goal and has the best opportunity for scoring and drawing ejections from over-zealous guards. The two-meter player must have the ability to shoot under physical duress with a defender behind, in front, or on either side. The two-meter player must recognize and understand the role of the other players, especially the drivers. Outstanding water polo teams are built around the two-meter player, the goalie and the two-meter guard. The two-meter player must be able to control the ball, shoot the ball despite intense physical contact, hold position in front of the goal, and accurately pass to teammates. Excellent swimming skills, overall strength, leg support and an ability to control his temper are all desired attributes in a two-meter player. This is, without a doubt, the most physically challenging position. Most teams develop at least two players for the two-meter position.

The front court offense has to be designed to help get the ball to the two-meter player. Three basic drives must be included in the front court offense:

- Drive to clear the area in front of the two-meter player so the ball can be received (a variety of drives may be necessary).

- Drive to get free to pass back or shoot.

- Drive to get inside water and a drive-in shot.

Because the rules make it difficult for drivers to determine when the two-meter player foul is being called, the designated driver(s) should begin moving slowly at first and then, on the whistle, accelerate to get free. Drivers should be aware of the referee's style of officiating. Some referees call a quick foul; others do not. Understanding this will give the drivers a better opportunity to anticipate potential foul situations.

#79 TWO-METER SHOTS WITH GUARD DRILL

Objective: To improve the two-meter player's ability to react to his defender's position, while emphasizing his need to perfect a variety of shots.

Description: A player passes to the two-meter player while the defender plays a token defense. The two-meter player receives the pass and shoots, using a variety of shots.

Variations: The defender may apply more pressure, specifically, hold and sink, while the two-meter player attempts to stay up and shoot. The two-meter player may also use turning moves.

Coaching Point:

- This drill should produce between 70 and 100 shots.

guard behind on right shoulder	guard behind on left shoulder	guard directly behind	guard right side	guard on left side	guard pushed out 2m inside water ball from corner	guard pushed out 2m inside water ball from opponents corner

#80 DIFFERENT ANGLE PASSING TO THE
TWO-METER PLAYER DRILL

Objective: To improve the ability of the two-meter player to receive passes from different positions and execute a variety of shots.

Description: No defenders are used in this drill. The two-meter player sets up along the two-meter line. The player moves to face incoming passes from different locations and takes a series of shots. Player resets himself in different spots in front of the goal.

Variation: A variety of shots may be used including: tip shots, backhands, turns, spins, and step-outs.

Coaching Point:

- The two-meter players should practice shooting during every practice. It is important that they practice getting their shots off quickly.

- Emphasize keeping the non-shooting arm out of the water to encourage the two-meter player to use his legs.

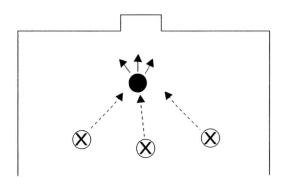

#81 ABSORB FOUL AND SHOOT DRILL

Objective: To improve the ability of the two-meter player to hold position even after being fouled, and to stay alert for another pass and opportunity to score.

Description: The ball is passed to the two-meter player who holds his position while being vigorously fouled. The coach blows the whistle to indicate a foul. The two-meter player releases to the outside passer who practices moving and then returns the ball. When the ball is passed to the two-meter player a third time, there is no whistle and he attempts a shot.

Variations: The coach may put a guard on the release player allowing one pass from a free throw, the other two with defensive pressure. The same drill can be run with the two-meter player on the right post or left post.

Coaching Points:

- The two-meter player must keep his guard behind him.

- As the players become more proficient at this drill, the coach may increase the pressure.

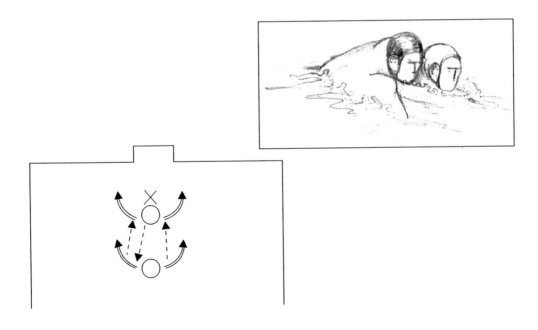

#82 PERIMETER PASS AND SHOOT DRILL

Objective: To improve quick releases on shots and passes.

Description: No defense, except the goalie. A pass is made to the two-meter player as the coach whistles to simulate a foul. The two-meter player immediately passes to any of the five perimeter players, who then passes to a third player who catches and shoots the ball in one motion.

Variations: The two-meter player should be set in different locations along the two- to three-meter line. Another pass can be added to this drill.

Coaching Points:

- If a poor pass is made, the ball returns to the two-meter player rather than being shot or passed.

- The release pass to the perimeter player must be accurate so that the player can catch and shoot in one motion.

- Perimeter players must be ready to receive the pass and shoot, and should constantly be watching the goalie's movement and position.

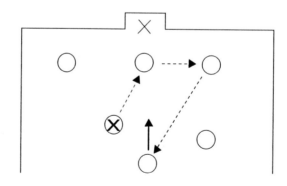

#83 REAR-BACK (RB) PASS FROM THE TWO-METER PLAYER DRILL

Objective: To improve the driver's rear-back (RB) catching and shooting ability.

Description: Three players line up along the 5- to 6-meter line. The two-meter player alternates passing to each driver along the line. Each driver rears back to receive the pass and shoot. This drill should also be practiced using "The Gareeni" (named after a very successful Italian player who, with no body movement and while staying low in the water to receive the pass from the two-meter player, would catch and shoot in one quick motion).

Variation: Same drill with two-meter player on opposite side.

Coaching Point:

- This drill can lead to similar shots being taken in the front court offense or during transition.

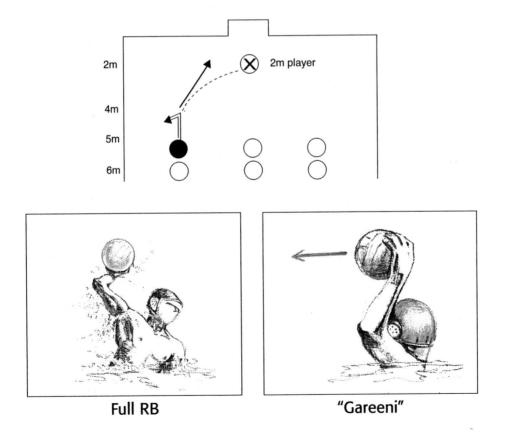

Full RB　　　　　　　"Gareeni"

#84 MOVING PICK DRILL

Objective: To improve proficiency in using picks and screens to free a player.

Description: In the first drill (Diagram A) player one crosses in front of player two, swimming slowly while in the screening position. Player one then accelerates toward the two-meter line and the two-meter player feeds him the ball. Player two crosses over the hips of player one and drives down to the two-meter line and the two-meter player passes him a second ball.

Variations: One variation (Diagram B) repeats the same drill except player two holds the outside position after player one has screened for him and RBs receiving a pass from the two-meter player. Another variation (Diagram C) repeats the first drill with the players interchanging on the wings. This variation gives the two-meter player the option of passing to the wings or players one and two. These drills can be practiced with defensive players.

Coaching Point:

- If player one is right-handed, different shots can be used, such as tips and RBs. Consequently, the same applies to player two in the first drill. These drills lead up to a front court offense.

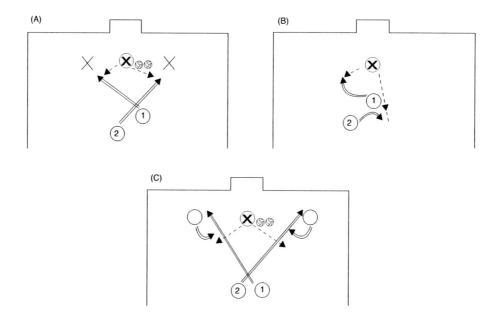

#85 WING PICK DRILL

Objective: To practice creating movement and freeing up players to receive passes from the two-meter player for a shot or release pass.

Description: Player one initiates the drive from the top outside wing and player two drives and screens off on player one's hips. Both go forward to receive the pass from the two-meter player (Diagram A). Continue the same drill but add deep wings for interchange movement in the pocket of the release pass (Diagram B).

Variations: Player one can hold for an RB or release the pass back to the two-meter player. Defensive players can be used in a half court controlled scrimmage. Same drill as the first except deep wings are added for interchange movement in the pocket of the release pass.

Coaching Points:

- Different shots, including tips and RBs, can be used if player one is right-handed. Consequently, the same applies to player two in the first drill.

- These drills lead up to a front court offense.

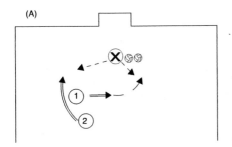

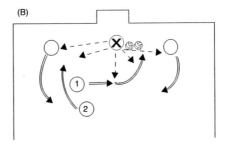

#86 THREE-ON-THREE FRONT COURT SCRIMMAGE DRILL

Objective: To practice recognizing passing and shooting opportunities while emphasizing motion in front of the goal.

Description: This drill uses three offensive players and three defenders plus a goalie in the front court. Start with an offensive player on the outside with the ball. On the coach's whistle, and with his back to the goal, that player puts the ball in play while the defender attacks with the proper defense. Passes are made to the two-meter player or other outside players. To create opportunities, offensive players should use "pass and go" inside moves to beat their defenders, or RB for a pass or shot.

Variation: The ball may start with the two-meter player.

Coaching Point:

- After each attempted shot, the coach resets the situation. Normal fouls should be called in order to facilitate "quickness."

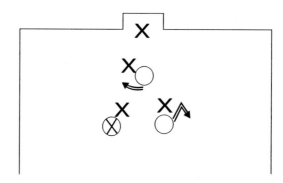

#87 FOUR-ON-FOUR FULL COURT SCRIMMAGE DRILL

Objective: To practice game situations in a highly competitive scrimmage that emphasizes the ability to make quick decisions. Quick ejections mean four-on-three opportunities.

Description: This scrimmage starts with a sprint from both ends of the 25-meter course.

Variations: A number of variations may be used, such as winners out (the team that scores gets the ball back), and counterattack scrimmage (whether a team scores or not, there is an immediate counterattack). Ejections are quick, with the player swimming and touching the goal post and returning.

Coaching Points:

- Four-on-four more closely resembles game situations, including team balance, that occur in a 30-meter course.

- This drill is an excellent physical conditioner that produces many different front court situations.

- The ejections allow for quick four-on-three opportunities.

- This is the foremost drill to help players understand game situations.

- This drill helps coaches evaluate the abilities of their players.

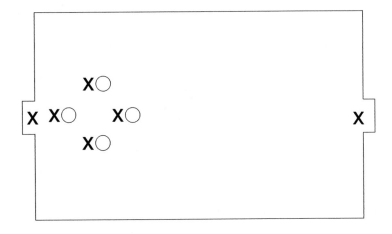

#88 FOUR PLAYER PASS AND TWO-METER RELEASE DRILL

Objective: To improve the two-meter player's ability to hold position and, if fouled, to pass quickly out to a teammate.

Description: The two-meter player starts by receiving a pass from the left. He locks in and holds position until the coach whistles a foul. The two-meter player then picks up the ball from underneath, lifts it quickly over his head and passes it back out to a perimeter player. He then works from left to right and repeats right to left, receiving passes while being defended at three-quarter speed.

Variation: Use defenders on the perimeter players. Offensive players must move, get free and RB back for the release from the two-meter player.

Coaching Point:

- Rarely should the two-meter player shovel pass directly from the water. Only in situations where a clear passing lane is open, and never over the head of a defender.

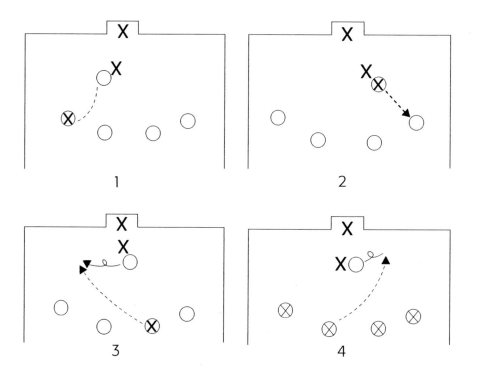

#89 THREE SECOND SCRIMMAGE DRILL

Objective: To improve motion anticipation while passing and receiving, with emphasis on situation recognition and quickness.

Description: Regular scrimmage except that individual players are only allowed to hold the ball for three seconds. They must pass or shoot within that time limit or the ball is turned over to the other team.

Variation: The team that scores gets the ball back. If a player is not guarded or touched by an opponent he can hold the ball longer. If a goal is scored, the goalie puts the ball back into play immediately – no stopping the scrimmage.

Coaching Points:

- This drill is only good for a limited time. Players eventually will get disorganized and play off their man too much.

- Emphasize that the players be aware of where the ball is at all times.

#90 NO FOUL SCRIMMAGE DRILL

Objective: To train players to make the extra effort needed while being closely guarded.

Description: Regular scrimmage except that no fouls are called.

Coaching Points:

- Coach must exert considerable control so that the physical part of the scrimmage does not get out of hand. The players must be instructed to not use elbows, fists, etc. Only holding is allowed, no sinking.

- The object is to see who gives the "extra effort."

#91 THREE MINUTE GAME SITUATION SCRIMMAGE DRILL

Objective: To train players to understand situations during a game when the team is ahead with three minutes to play or behind with three minutes to play.

Description: Regular scrimmage, using the time clock and all the necessary equipment for a formal game, including referees.

Coaching Point:

- The coach determines the difference in the score. At the end of each three minute situation, the coach and team discuss and evaluate performance and strategy. Note: This should not be done more than once every two weeks during the season, because there is usually too much emphasis on what not to do, rather than on what to do.

#92 HALF COURT TIMING DRILL

Objective: To improve team coordination and concentration.

Description: Drill begins with six balls and 12 players arranged with three players in each "corner." Four players at a time coordinate their movements so that an uninterrupted sequence of passes results in a shot on goal (outside five meters). There should be no delay, no fakes, no waiting to receive the ball. Every player must call for the ball, or he should not be passed to.

Variation: This drill can be run in the reverse direction so that the right-handed shooter receives the cross pass. It can also be a workout drill with more players (20 max). You can have penalties such as push-ups when a player doesn't call for the ball, makes a bad pass, or misses a shot.

Coaching Point:

- This drill is a good pre-game warm-up for the entire squad. It helps the team synchronize and emphasizes visual and verbal communication.

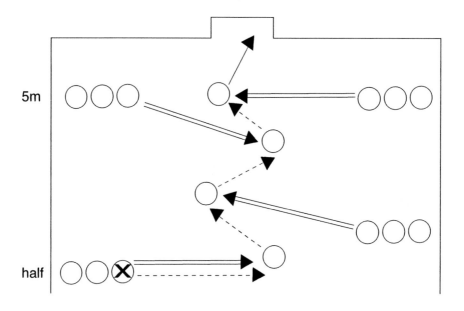

CHAPTER 8

SIX-ON-FIVE
EXTRA PLAYER BASICS

INTRODUCTION

SIX-ON-FIVE OFFENSE

There are two basic offensive systems: the 4-2 and the 3-3. In this chapter are several variations and rotations of these two formations. An important point to be considered is the time available to set up the offense. For example, the twenty seconds man-up situation means an aggressive attack must be mounted in order to have a scoring opportunity. Each system has its advantages and disadvantages. The 3-3 is important because when there is enough time to set it up (such as when an ejection is in the back court), a quick 3-3 with shorter passes is desirable. the 3-3 formation may also be the best, if a team has less experienced players. A variety of numbering systems can be used, but a basic one is the following:

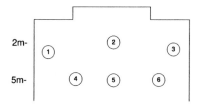

The 3-3 formation is the most vulnerable to counterattack. Whichever system is used, the fundamental principal to remember is to look for a quick opportunity, then look for opportunities for the players on the 2-meter line at the post positions.

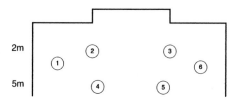

The advantage with the 4-2 formation is that having four players along the 2-meter line forces the goalie to move a greater distance to cover all of them. Also, rotations that include players 1 and 6 taking the ball inside two meters gets the offensive team that follows closer to the goal, giving them a better opportunity to score. Disadvantages include the longer length of time it takes to set up, the need for more experienced players because longer passes are required, and the need for all of the players to be scorers.

#93 BASIC LINE-UP FORMATIONS DRILL

Objective: To practice the basic movements in a six-on-five offense.

Descriptions: These are basic line-ups and pairings for six-on-five power plays. Players six and two line up and move together, as do players one and three. Players four and five remain parallel. The positions are determined by the player with the ball. Specifically, when players one or six have the ball. Practice passing from player six to player two and player one to player three.

Variation: The defenders are staged so that players can recognize openings.

Coaching Points:

- The moving ball is based on short and/or long triangles. Emphasize catching and shooting rather than faking and shooting. If using a fake, it should be a body fake and not an arm fake.

- This is the foundation of extra man. Variations in the formations will depend on the abilities and types of players available.

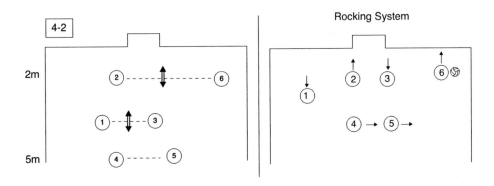

Basic Movements for Getting Open for Passes

Players 6 & 2 line up and move together
Players 1 & 3 Line up and move together
Players 4 & 5 stay parallel

Note: The player with the ball dictates position - specifcally players 1 & 6.

#94 PERIMETER PASSING AND SHOOTING DRILL

Objective: To improve passing and shooting skills while learning to create shooting opportunities by moving the goalie.

Description: The pass can start at either player one or player six. One to five passes are completed before a shot is taken.

Variations: Use the Pass 6-5-4-1 before shooting, using the big body fake (no pump fakes) as if to shoot but pass instead. After the ball gets to player one, make up to three more passes and then shoot. Another variation is to start this same series of passes but shoot at any time if the goal appears to be open.

Coaching Points:

- Ball movement is based on short and/or long triangles. Emphasize catching and shooting rather than arm/hand faking and shooting. A body fake should be used, not an arm fake.

- A perimeter pass with the proper body motion fake gets zone defenders and goalie out of position.

- When passing to a teammate there should be minimal spin on the ball. This means the passer must come up higher in the water. When shooting, however, use lots of spin on the ball.

- A body fake is when the player comes up high from the water and turns his non-shooting arm towards the goal. The ball is taken far back in the body rotation and in a sweeping action that looks like a shot, is passed to a teammate.

- Emphasize that the body does not lean back.

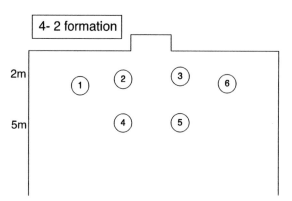

#95 NEAR TRIANGLES DRILL

Objective: To practice creating shooting opportunities.

Description: Near triangle passes force defenders to move against a three-on-two on each side and eventually get out of position. The drill starts with a pass from player one or player six. Practice at two different goals. Players pass back and forth within each near triangle and take a shot every two to five passes.

Variations: Put in a center defender and one opposite post player. This way if the center defender moves to one post, the other is open. Same drill using long triangles to make the goalie and zone defense move even farther.

Coaching Point:

- Moving the ball is based on short and/or long triangles. Emphasize catching and shooting rather than faking and shooting. A body fake should be used, not an arm fake.

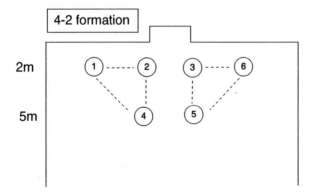

#96 BOX-POSTS PASS DRILL

Objective: To practice recognizing when players two and three are open for passes from players four and five.

Description: Players four and five should pass back and forth and then hit players two or three with a quick pass. Players two and three should be ready to either catch and pass, shoot, or tip the ball.

Variations: Use the passing sequence 5-3-1 or 4-2-3. Passes may include five to three to two or four to two to three. Defenders should be positioned between passers.

Coaching Point:

- Coaches should stress recognition of posts. If a quick shot is not available, this is the area that should be looked at first.

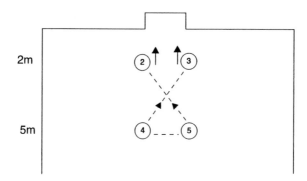

#97 BASELINE DRILL

Objective: To practice recognizing movement and passing opportunities in the 4-2 formation during a six-on-five.

Description: This drill involves only the bottom line of the 4-2 formation. Only passes to players two and three from players one and six are practiced. On a pass from six to three, player three shoots across the cage on a pop-out. On a pass from one to three, player three uses a backhand push or tip shot. When player two receives a pass from player one, he shoots backhand to the near corner. If player two is left handed, he shoots a cross-goal shot on a pass from one, and a near-corner shot on a pass from six. If player three is left handed he shoots a near-corner shot on a pass from player one and a tip or cross-goal shot on a pass from player six.

Variation: The coach may put three defenders in and make the players stay in the basic 4-2 formation.

Coaching Point:

- When using defenders, this drill will give players two and three more practice shots and improve their ability to recognize openings.

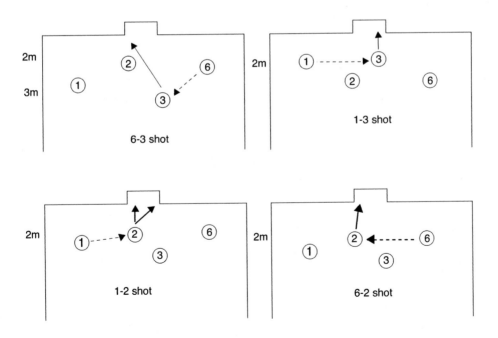

#98 ONE-TO-SIX PASS DRILL

Objective: To practice long passes in the 4-2 formation in order to force goalie movement.

Description: Besides players one and six passing to players two and three, one and six can pass to each other. The one-six pass is a difficult pass and requires skilled players to make a successful pass. Simple passing back and forth will get the goalie out of position for a shot. Occasionally, pass to two or three. Line up one and six on the three-meter line, with players two and three on the four-meter line.

Variation: Use positions four and five every third pass.

Coaching Points:

- Too often, by the third pass, a player will over pass his teammate.
- Look for passing lanes, do not pass over the defender's heads.
- Players should rotate positions.

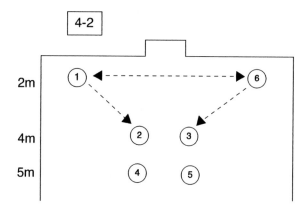

#99 OUTSIDE THREE PLAYERS PASSING AND SHOOTING DRILL

Objective: To improve passing and shooting skills from outside six meters.

Description: Three players line up along the six-meter line. The players pass back and forth and take shots.

Variation: Place two defenders between the three offensive players. Should the defenders intercept a pass, then the player who threw the interception and his intended receiver go on defense.

Coaching Points:

- This drill is not only for six-on-five shooting, it is also effective for a 3-3 formation, against a drop back and as part of a front court offense.

- Without defenders, limit passes to a maximum of three and then a shot.

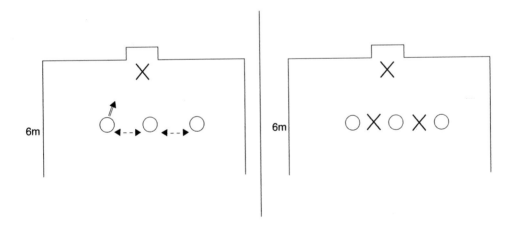

#100 HUNGARIAN SHOOTING DRILL

Objective: To practice creating passing and shooting opportunities in extra man situations.

Description: This drill can be set up in either a 3-3 or 4-2 formation, with a goalie. At least five extra water polo balls will be used. The first shooter chases his shot and, after making sure that he is outside the two-meter line, comes up in the water and passes to any other player. He then immediately returns to his original position. The receiver then shoots and repeats this same action. (He may get the ball nearest to him to pass.) All players must stay alert and be ready to shoot, always aware of the goalie's position. Positions rotate every three minutes until all players have played all positions.

Variation: Players must add a pass before each shot.

Coaching Points:

- This is the most definitive drill for extra player awareness and shot availability.

- Make sure that the player's reactions to chase the ball are quick and the shooter chases and passes from outside the two-meter line, quickly returning to his original position.

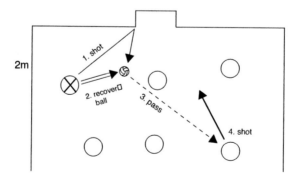

#101 SIX-ON-FIVE THEN RED HAT COUNTERATTACK DRILL

Objective: To improve concentration and scoring opportunities in a six-on-five.

Description: This drill begins with a six-player team on offense and a five-player team on defense. If the offensive team scores, they stay on offense. The defensive team has an extra player outside, on the two-meter line. If the offensive team misses, then a counter occurs with the extra defensive player (wearing a red hat) actively involved in countering to the other goal. The defenders become the offense and the offense becomes the defense, with their sixth player (also in a red hat) off to the side until they are ready to counterattack. Formation can be either a 3-3 or 4-2.

Variation: This drill can be effective in both the 30-meter and 25-meter course.

Coaching Points:

- Give each team five minutes to prepare. Team members should use this time to communicate with each other.

- Change "red hat" players every five minutes.

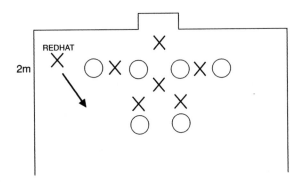

List of Terms

Back Door: An offensive drive from the wing position on the weakside (away from the ball).

Backhand Shot: Shot toward the goal while facing away from the goal.

Balance: While in a vertical position, keeping the body steady so a pass can be received or a shot taken with accuracy.

Ball Control: Offensive team maintains possession of the ball.

Body Fake: In passing, using the chest and upper body rotation so the pass looks like a shot.

Breakaway: When a player completely breaks away from the defense.

Cage: Another name for the water polo goal.

Circle Pass Drills: A series of passing drills with players formed in a circle.

Counter Rotate: During a counterattack, movement by players rotating away from the ball.

Counterattack: A fast break with players switching from defense to offense.

Crashing: Perimeter defenders dropping back quickly on a two-meter player with the ball.

Cross-face Pass: Ball is received across the face of a player.

Cross Over Backhand Pass/Shot: Rolling a hand over the ball and passing or shooting while facing away from the receiver or the goal.

Drive: An effort to swim past the defensive player.

Drive-in Shots: Shots taken by the driver.

Drop Back Defense: A zone or man-to-man defense where defensive players drop back off of the offensive perimeter players.

Dry Pass: Pass from one player to another without the ball touching the water.

Dribble: To swim with the ball in front of one's face, using the crawl arm stroke to keep the ball.

Eggbeater: An alternating breaststroke type of kick.

Ejection: When a player is removed for committing a major foul.

Eleven O'Clock: Far left outside position in a 3-3 formation.

Eye-to-Eye Contact: Offensive players looking directly at each other before a pass is made.

Eternity Drills: A drill that can be extended for an indefinite period of time.

Extra-man: An ejection (personal foul) of a player that enables the offensive team to have an extra player advantage, (6-on-5). Also, player up situations: two on one, three on two, etc.

Face-off: Like a jump ball, the official tosses a ball between offensive and defensive players who each attempt to gain possession of the ball.

FINA: Federation Internationale de Natation Amateur: An international governing aquatic body for diving, synchronized swimming, swimming and water polo.

Five-on-Six: The defensive line-up when a team has lost a player.

Forcing the ball: Trying to pass the ball past a defender or into an area that is being guarded.

Foul and Drop: When a defensive player commits a foul to slow play so he can drop back to defend an offensive player closer to the goal.

Four-two (4-2): The line-up for attacking a five-player defense, including extra-player and counterattack.

Front Court (Ft): The offensive half of the playing field (pool).

Front Water: When an offensive player has no defender between him and the defensive goal.

Gareeni Shot: A ball that is caught and immediately shot without noticeable body movement by the shooter.

Goalie or Goal Keeper: A designated player who defends the goal.

Grab Block: While an offensive player with the ball is in the process of passing, the defender grabs him around the waist and pulls him underwater and toward the defender.

Hesitation Drive: An attempt to get the defensive player off balance so a drive can be made.

High Water Polo: Pertains to alertness, staying high in the water.

Hole: Area in front of the cage.

Holeman: The player in the hole area (usually the two-meter player).

Hook: The act of turning – usually refers to right-angle moves or bow outs.

Hungarian Drill: A 6-on-5 drill devised by the Hungarian National Team.

Intensity Shooting Drills: Drills that involve extreme physical effort in regard to multiple shots by one person.

Inside: Offensive player gets in front of the defender.

Inside Water: Anywhere in the pool where an offensive player is ahead of the defender.

Kick Out: An ejection.

Lanes: Areas free of defenders arms, allowing safe passes, and/or areas into which defensive players move.

Layout Shot: Laying flat on one's back and shooting, (can also be a method of passing).

Lead Break: The players that reach the offensive end first.

Lunge Block: Matching hands of passer and pushing down.

Match Hands: Right to left – left to right matching of defender's hands to the shooters.

Mobility Drills: Drills that include movement and swimming.

Moving Pick: Moving screen intended to free an offensive player for a release pass and/or shot.

Natural Goals: Goals scored when both teams have an even number of players.

Off Water Shot: A shot that is taken from the water.

Offensive Foul: Foul committed by an offensive player.

One O'Clock: Far right outside position in a 3-3 formation.

Pass and Go: Player passes then immediately drives.

Passing Lanes: Clear passing areas between offensive players.

Penalty Shot: Free shot at goal from the four-meter line.

Perimeter Passing: Usually refers to passing during a 6-on-5 situation or against a zone.

Pick: An offensive move to screen defenders away from the shooter.

Point: The position at the top of the offensive set-up in the center of the pool.

Pop Shot: Player lifts the ball with one hand and shoots the ball into the goal with the other hand.

Pull Back: An ejection foul when an offensive player, who is beating his defender, is pulled back by the defender.

Pump Ball: Faking as if to shoot.

Quicks: Referring to quick shots.

RB: Player stops quickly and rears up and back to receive the ball.

Rear Back: Same as RB.

Roll-and-Pass: Body rolls in a layout position, right to left or left to right.

Screw-shot: A drive-in shot using one hand to reach under the ball and, while rotating the wrist, bring the ball up to the shoulder and shoot.

Second Pass Counterattack: Lead break gets to the two-meter line while a pass is made to the half-court player who then passes to the lead break player.

Seesaw Passing: Coming up high in the water to receive the ball and again to pass the ball.

Sequential Wings: The timing of passes to players who are making wings to advance the ball.

Six-on-Five: A one-player advantage situation.

Stop-and-go: Attempting to get free from a player by stopping and going.

Strongside: The side of the pool where the ball is located.

Switch: Defenders switching defensive responsibilities.

Team Balance: An offensive formation for a team that enables it to successfully run its offense.

Three-three (3-3): Three players along the two-meter line and three players usually between the five- and six-meter line. Counterattack or extra player offense.

Timing Pass: Pass thrown in rhythm with another player, so he does not have to stop swimming or moving.

Transition: Going from defense to offense, or offense to defense.

Triangle: Offensive formation for a counterattack or for right or left 6-on-5 formations.

Triangle Passing: Referring to a 6-on-5 formation and the direction of passes on the perimeter.

Turn-over: Losing the ball to the other team.

Two-meter Defender: The guard on the two-meter player.

Two-meter Player: Holeman/player in front of the goal, who is the center of the offense.

Two-meter Shots: Shots taken by the two-meter player.

Two-meter Line: The line at each end of the pool where the offensive player is not allowed, unless the ball is inside or the player himself takes the ball into that area.

Walk: Pertains to players in drills using the eggbeater kick to go across the pool.

Weakside: The side of the pool away from the ball.

Wet Pass: A pass from one player to another that lands in the water near the receiver.

Wet Shot: A shot that is attempted while the ball is controlled in the water. This is also called an off the water shot.

Wing: Players position on each side of pool, front court or goal.

Zone Defense: Either a five-player zone against a six-player offense or a six-player zone defense.

25m: 25-meter pool length (women's field of play).

30m: 30-meter pool length. Also, the official length for high school, college and international water polo.

Peter J. Cutino is the all-time winningest coach, combined with NCAA and United States club championships, in the history of the sport of water polo in the United States. In his illustrious career, his teams won twenty-one national championships, including eight NCAA Championships (the most in NCAA water polo history).

A graduate of California State Polytechnic University in San Luis Obispo, where he was an outstanding athlete in three sports (water polo, swimming, and basketball), Peter began his renowned coaching career as the head swimming and water polo coach at Oxnard (CA) High School in 1957. In six seasons, his swimming teams won two California Interscholastic Federation Championships, five league championships, and sixty dual meets in a row. Concurrently, his water polo teams compiled an 87-8 record during that period.

In 1963, Peter was head varsity swimming and water polo coach at the University of California – Berkeley. Subsequently, he spent eleven years as the mentor of the swimming program. He served as the water polo coach for 26 seasons. During his tenure, his water polo teams accorded a remarkable 519 – 172 record. In the process, Peter was named "Water Polo Coach of the Year" on fifteen occasions by a distinguished array of collegiate, national, and international organizations. His coaching achievements are further reflected in the fact that he has been named to seven different athletic-related Halls of Fame, including The National Water Polo Hall of Fame in 1995. Perhaps his greatest honor occurred when the award given annually to the best men's and women's intercollegiate water polo player was named the Pete Cutino Award (the equivalent of the Heisman Trophy and the Wooden Award in football and basketball, respectively).

Peter and his wife, Louise, currently reside in Monterey, California. They have three grown children – Paul Joseph, Peter John, and Anna Marie.

Peter Cutino Jr. is currently an architect with G.T.P. Consultants in Seville, Spain. He is a 1984 graduate of the University of California, Berkeley, where he had a distinguished career as a water polo player. A two-time All-American on the Bears' water polo team, he helped lead Cal to the NCAA National Championship in 1983. In the process, he earned several honors, including being named Pac-10 Conference Player of the Year, NCAA Collegiate Co-Player of the Year, and co-MVP of the NCAA Tournament. As an athlete, he frequently participated in international competition in water polo during the period 1980 – 1987.

Peter began his coaching career in 1979, working as an age group coach for the Concord Water Polo Club. Beginning in 1984, he served as an assistant coach for his alma mater's water polo team for three seasons. Since 1988, he has been the head coach of The Seville national club team – a team which has won ten regional championships under his tutelage. In 1993, he founded the Seville Water Polo Foundation, an organization for which he currently serves as President.

Peter and his wife, Marisol, currently reside in Seville, Spain with their two children, Peter and Paolo.